I0185290

The author shares her journey of transformation in the wisdom pathway of Ke Ala Hōkū through intensive studies with Kahuna (Native Hawaiian spiritual practitioner) Abraham Kawai'i, who chose to open these ancient teachings to people outside of his culture.

The principles of this work offer profound indigenous wisdom, guiding us to restore our relationship with the consciousness that infuses all of Life. It introduces us to "the ancient soul of the body" – the meeting place of matter and spirit inside our cells.

Awakening the Ancient Soul of the Body is an invitation to look beyond our common separation of body, mind, and spirit and remember our intrinsic wholeness. These principles guide us in a unique experience of restoring our original identity as "a light-filled intelligence, far beyond the conscious mind," and our relationship with our 'Ohana Nui – The Great Family of All Life.

Jody Mountain

Ke Ala Hōkū – The Pathway to The Stars

Awakening the Ancient Soul of the Body

Copyright © 2023 Jody Mountain. All rights reserved.

No part of this publication, including illustrations and artwork, may be reproduced in any form, or by any means, electronic or physical, without written permission from the copyright holder except in brief quotations in critical articles and reviews.

Contact: www.LineageofLight.com

First paperback edition: May, 2023

ISBN-13: 979-8-218-19766-7 (Paperback Book)

DISCLAIMER
This book is distributed and sold with the understanding that the author is not hereby engaged in the delivery of any medical or psychological advice, service, or treatment. Individuals are advised to consult a healthcare professional should their own life circumstances warrant personal attention. The author disclaims any liability arising directly or indirectly from the use and application of any of the book's contents.

Artwork by Sarina Heinzmann
Book and cover design by Jody Mountain
Format Design by Luca Blum
Edited by Jeff Braucher

A portion of the proceeds of the sale of this book will be donated to benefit the family of Kahu Abraham Kawai'i.

This book, and every moment of my life, I owe to my Ancestors. To my parents who gave me the Life that has continued to blossom in such miraculous ways, thank you for your profound guidance and example of how to live from Love.

I offer this book in the deepest gratitude to my teacher, Kahu Abraham Kawai'i, Aua'ia, Maka'i'ole, 'uliama, to his wife, Ho'okahi, a potent teacher in her own right, and to the Sacred Beloved Spirit in all things. May this Pathway be a blessing to all who receive it.

Contents

Preface 11

Introduction 13

Chapter 1 – Stepping Across the Line 21

Chapter 2 – The Body Is Alive 29

Chapter 3 – 'Ohana Nui, The Great Family 37

Chapter 4 – Internal Navigation 47

Chapter 5 – Our Perceptive Field 57

Chapter 6 – Center of Our Universe 67

Chapter 7 – Ho'oponopono 77

Chapter 8 – Ancient Lomi Lomi 85

Chapter 9 – Resonance of a New Paradigm 93

Integration Exercises 101

Acknowledgments 116

Glossary 120

PREFACE

Ke Ala Hōkū – The Pathway to the Stars, is a body of rare Wisdom Teachings from far-ancient Hawai'i. For the Hawaiian people, who can trace their lineage back to the Pleiades, Ke Ala Hōkū is the pathway home.

For the rest of us, Ke Ala Hōkū offers a pathway back to our indigenous roots, returning us to our original communion with Life Itself.

In ancient times, this pathway called for extensive training to open mystical depths of awareness both inside and out. Its culmination involved ritual and ceremony, known as Lomi Ke a Hōkū, a form of bodywork that attended to the body as a living expression of the Sacred.

The work came to me through my teacher, Kahu Abraham Kawai'i, a Hawaiian Kahuna (Master) who traced his lineage back through the original inhabitants of the Hawaiian Islands. Kahu became a Kahuna of nine diverse streams of ancient wisdom in which he saw the common foundation from which everything springs. The Pathway Home is the pathway back to our original state of being. It is the pathway back to our original relationship with ourselves, with others, with our families, with our communities and with all of Life.

This book contains some of the sacred teachings Kahu chose to share outside of his culture. His willingness to offer his wisdom to a wider community has caused much controversy in some Hawaiian communities. Nevertheless, I believe that Kahu chose to share these teachings widely because he could foresee a time when this Pathway would be needed by many on Earth. He realized that, at its foundational level, the work is beyond culture and tradition, and that it could be ignited in any human who has the willingness to go beyond their existing perceptions of themselves and the world around them.

In his words: "It is not a matter of blood, it is a matter of Spirit."

He transmitted the work not just through the Universal Principles at their core, but through embodied experience. Students found themselves in motion with the

Principles, which led them to face their inner and outer worlds in new ways. Each person's learning then, was a unique unfolding which arose from inside of them as they walked a new path.

In its modern form, Ke Ala Hōkū calls us to uncover realms within ourselves that are not generally accessible in our present-day lives. It brings to our conscious experience, dimensions of hidden possibility that have existed in us since the beginning of time.

The Pathway to the Stars guides us through the layers of our learned perceptions and allows us to open to the pure Life that inhabits our every cell. It restores our lineage as inherently sacred beings and awakens the Ancient Soul of the Body.

INTRODUCTION

The night sky was black. No moon, no stars. There was stillness in the air. The sound of an occasional bird rang out from the darkness. Five tents were pitched close to the shoreline of the Pacific Ocean, the inhabitants in deep slumber.

Inside one of the tents, the Kahuna teacher began to stir. He rose, quietly gathered his supplies, loaded a nearby canoe, and sounded the call for everyone to wake up.

The students rose quickly. The master ordered them into the canoe and began paddling steadily away from shore. After some time, he commanded, "Everyone in the water." Without hesitation, the students jumped overboard into the dark sea. "Your task is to find your way back to shore."

In the pitch blackness, with no light from above, and no lights on the shoreline, their best option was to follow the sound of the canoe paddle as their teacher returned to shore. As they listened for the sound, however, they could hear no paddling. The Kahuna was letting his canoe rest in the waves, allowing them to carry him back to shore. The students began to listen keenly to see if they could decipher the sound of the waves lapping onto the sides of the canoe. Instead, they began to hear the sounds of great thrashing.

The water was suddenly churning with sharks. Catching a strong scent in the air, the students soon realized that the master had begun to pour a bucket of pig's blood into the water, inevitably attracting these powerful creatures during their prime feeding time. Returning to shore meant following the sharks who would be closely behind their teacher's canoe.

A potential challenge of skill and stamina had become a test of life or death.

This was one of the tests undertaken by my teacher. His task was to find the way back to shore in the midst of a feeding frenzy of hungry sharks. Every fiber of his being had to know, beyond any doubt, that the very same Life was alive in each of them. He had to know this in his cells, in his emotions, and in the vibration that poured through him. If his whole being was in resonance with Life, the sharks would perceive him as one of them, and he could remain in the water, swimming beside them, unharmed.

In this particular stream of study, though not in all Hawaiian wisdom lineages, initiates would undergo sometimes numerous life or death tests before being recognized as Kahuna. The actual number they would face depended on their teacher. If they survived, they would be considered Masters in their field of study. If they didn't, they would not be alive to pass on only partial truths.

The word *Kahuna* in Hawaiian culture means, in one translation, "Keeper of the Secret". It describes people who trained deeply in a certain field of knowledge, acquiring the depths of understanding and insight that come with decades of training. In ancient times there were Kāhuna of such diverse fields as architecture, fishing, sculpture, bone setting, midwifery, canoe building, navigation, health diagnostics, Lomi Lomi (Hawaiian massage), and herbal medicine, among many others. Sometimes two or three related streams of knowledge that might complement each other would be offered.

My teacher, Kahu, studied with nine different experts, making him the recipient of an unusual number of diverse streams of knowledge. Kahu's family, as well as each of his teachers, trace their wisdom lineages back to the original indigenous inhabitants of Hawai'i.

What most know as a vacation paradise was once The Kingdom of Hawai'i, an internationally recognized sovereign nation populated by several waves of Polynesian voyagers from French Polynesia, Tahiti, the Marquesas Islands, Tuamotus and the Samoan Islands. In 1893 the United States illegally occupied The Kingdom of Hawai'i, and overthrew overthrew the reigning monarch, Queen Lili'oukalani by force. The Kingdom of Hawai'i was declared an incorporated territory of the United States in 1900, and eventually became the State of Hawai'i in 1959.

According to Hawaiian mythology, prior to the arrival of the Polynesians, original inhabitants of a number of different races inhabited these islands. In *Beckwith's Hawaiian Mythology*, there are references to the most commonly known of these, the Menehune, originally called the Manahuna, and several other forest dwelling tribes, including the Nawao – who were hunters descended from Lua-nu'u, the Wa people, and People of the Mu. One of the only existing records show a census conducted in 1820 on the island of Kaua'i by Kaumuali'i, the Ali'i 'Aimoku (ruling Chief) of the island, which lists sixty-five people who identified their race as Menehune.

The indigenous peoples of Hawai'i were primarily agrarian. They were said to have magical abilities as healers in addition to being excellent builders and fishermen. The potent wisdom of these miraculous people was passed down through oral tradition, mentoring and apprenticeship. Eventually this knowledge became more and more hidden to protect its integrity.

All of Kahu's teachers carried wisdom from these ancient peoples, whose legacy extends prior to the arrival of Polynesian explorers, and beyond. In Kahu's words: "The origins of the work go back to Egypt, before it was called Egypt." Each of his lineages had chosen to preserve the ancient ways "underground" for safekeeping. In more recent times, it was preserved in spite of rapidly expanding belief systems like Christianity. All nine families of Kahu's healing lineage managed to preserve these sacred teachings in a largely unbroken line of transmission.

In ancient times, knowledge was passed from elder to offspring. The healing work of Lomi Lomi (Hawaiian massage) was cultivated through the expertise of many different families each choosing to hold the wisdom and further the practice of specific healing modalities. Some families developed a focus on the skeletal structure and passed down healing techniques such as bone setting. Others specialized in pregnancy and childbirth and developed healing practices to care for the health of baby and mother both during and after birth. Throughout the ages, the lineages of Lomi Lomi were born out of necessity to address different conditions in the body, mind and spirit. As it is most commonly taught today, many different lineages are combined to offer a wide spectrum of healing modalities to students.

Kahu's expertise included various streams of therapeutic Lomi Lomi such as bone setting and working with the needs of the musculoskeletal system for injury repair and general well-being. His lineages guided him also toward an expertise in mystical forms of Lomi Lomi, such as Lomi Ke Ala Hōkū. He was gifted in the art of Hawaiian Geomancy, and had experience in Lua (a Hawaiian martial art). Kahu also possessed the 'ike (wisdom knowledge) of Ke Ahi Pū and Ka Nu'u Mamao, the female and male versions of awakening Life Force energy, or what some would understand as Kundalini, among others. Through my experience of him, I understood Kahu to be a keeper of mystical wisdom.

His profound ability to synthesize and embody these streams of knowledge resulted in an expansive vision of healing. In his words: "The Kahuna Training develops deep simplicity through observation and application of oneself, of nature and natural rhythms, including the physical body. The concerns of that particular domain being the cellular structure and even further into molecular and atomic."

For most of his life, Kahu called the bodywork which he came to practice and teach: "Kahuna Bodywork." In the years before his passing in 2004, he called it Romi Kaparere, meaning 'to dance around the table'. Streams of this work flowing through some of his students go by names such as: Lomi Lomi Nui, Ancient Hawaiian Bodywork, Temple Style Bodywork and Kahuna Massage, among others.

The stream that seemed to 'land' in me through our time together is a facet of Kahuna Bodywork (Lomi Ke Ala Hōkū) which I feel is foundational. I experience it as an opening to the resonant life force moving through my body, through every aspect of who I am, and through all of Life. The Pathway to the Stars is this opening.

My journey toward this rare and ancient lineage of Hawaiian Wisdom began with a childhood in Jamaica, where I was immersed in movement and dance from the age of four. Looking back, it seems that I was enchanted with embodiment – the body as an engaging and dynamic interface with the world around me. Later my attention expanded to my internal interface. How did my mental, emotional, spiritual and ancestral aspects inhabit this particular combination of cells?

After moving to Canada with my family and completing university, I began to forge a career in choreography. My fascination with the body grew and gradually, I became interested in becoming a Massage Therapist. As fate or destiny would have it, I happened upon a lecture demonstration of "Ancient Hawaiian Bodywork". That experience was in itself an alchemical moment. It was such a pivotal event that I can clearly delineate who I was before and who I was after.

The event was hosted by a man named Patrick, a student of Kahu's who was traveling around North America teaching the work. At the presentation, Patrick talked about the history, principles, and application of the work. He spoke about the power of the present moment, how our perceptions shaped our world, and that we are not victims of our environment but rather powerful creators.

My jaw hit the floor. I had never encountered such ideas before, and yet I recognized truth after truth in his words. Each principle made more sense to me than anything I had ever heard. Every few sentences, my insides were bursting with yes! Yes! YES!

As he embarked on a stunning hands-on demonstration of the bodywork, a hush fell over the room. The combination of graceful, dancing movements, undulating rhythms, and powerful music was mesmerizing. Although I couldn't quite comprehend how, it seemed as if the recipients body was being massaged everywhere at once. My friend sitting beside me whispered, "Wow. What I wouldn't give to be on that table." All I wanted was to learn how to do it.

Diving in to five immersive trainings with Patrick, every previous ambition faded away. I was completely enthralled with the work. It was igniting an exploration of that internal interface I had glimpsed so long ago: What is the relationship between my cellular being and my mental, emotional, spiritual self? How much is ancestral programming? How much is what I've learned? How much is nature? What is my relationship to the nature around me and the nature inside of me?

In 1996, I found my way to the doorstep of the Kahuna himself. This training, and my subsequent encounters with Kahu forever changed what I understood the work to be. It began to permeate every aspect of my life. This Pathway essentially became my guiding principle.

Through Kahu, I discovered a vast reservoir of wisdom of which the bodywork was only a tiny piece. His teachings began the awakening of an ancient and lost part of myself that I didn't even know existed. To say it has been life-changing is an understatement. The work of Ke Ala Hōkū uprooted my old perceptions of myself and the world, revealing the living pulse of Creation in all that I experience.

My Soul as an etheric and disembodied idea dissolved, and in its place reemerged a sacred, ancient, embodied feeling that includes every aspect of who I am, and can barely be put into words. The essence of this voice says "Welcome home".

The journey is an ongoing one. Life continues to be a vibrant discovery of where I have been unconsciously limited, holding on to old patterns, or living in the past. As I meet each threshold, deeper and wider dimensions of possibility reveal themselves. This pathway has led to an ever-expanding shift in who I understand myself to be, and leaves me again and again, in a state of pure wonder. In this way, I consider myself a life-long student of the work.

To be clear, I am neither a Hawaiian Cultural Practitioner nor an expert in Hawaiian culture. Despite the depth of my training, I was only exposed to a fraction of Kahu's knowledge. It is clear to me that my path does not, and cannot, lead to becoming Kahuna. This is a title very few can claim, and is limited to those within Hawaiian bloodlines.

Awakening the Ancient Soul of the Body, is an opening to this Pathway. As you read, I encourage you to be aware of your body. Check in every once in a while to release any tension, relax your breath, and take in the ideas as you would a beautiful landscape, a rushing river, a full moon reflecting on the ocean, or a night sky full of stars. Invite an awareness of your essential being to be present as you read. Let yourself be immersed in the rhythm of the words, as if you were in the midst of a warm, quietly moving ocean. Let your analytical and associative mind relax in the knowing that these writings speak to places your conscious mind might not be able to reach or understand.

What follows is not a static truth, but rather my unique impressions and experiences on this transformational path. These include my impressions of my teacher, his guidance as I received it, and how Life has opened beyond my imagination. This accounting is my understanding of a work which likely has depths and layers of which I am not yet aware.

Ke Ala Hōkū has revealed itself as an infinite pathway bringing me perpetually back to the beginning, to meet a new dawn that is always breaking.

CHAPTER 1
STEPPING ACROSS THE LINE

THE SEEKER

There is a story about a Pilgrim in search of the Truth. He traveled to many sacred places and consulted many great masters, shamans, and wise ones. Finally, he found himself at the foot of a great mountain. After an arduous climb to the top, he was led to a reclusive Sage and asked his question for the final time:

"Master, if you could give me the one wisdom that would serve me in all of life's moments, no matter what the situation, what would it be?"

The Holy Man replied: *"Pay attention"*.

"If you are prepared to die, take a breath, be prepared, and step across this line."

These were the last words an initiate in ancient times would hear before they stepped into the *heiau* or temple to accept their destiny. Entering the small stone structure filled with offerings, torches, chanters, drummers, and a stone slab, the initiate would take their last breath of "the old" before being born into a new life.

Blinded by the heat of the fire and reverberating with the sounds of living prayer, the initiate was placed on the stone slab. Using their entire bodies in a rhythmic dance, the five Kāhuna, in combination or alone, would work on the initiate, weaving flesh, muscle, bone, sound, energy, breath, and light. The ceremony would continue for a minimum of ten hours, some lasting up to fifteen days, twenty-four hours per day.

The Kāhuna were engaged in a great remembering. Their cellular resonance became the embodiment of Life in all forms. Igniting their multi-dimensional attention, they became the ocean, wind, Earth, and stars. Their cells embodied the rhythms, colors, movements, energies, and frequencies of all of Life, calling out to that same Life inside the cells of their recipient.

The ceremony of Lomi Ke Ala Hōkū was offered only by special invitation. Initiates would undergo extensive questioning to determine their readiness. The transformational session was calling them back to their origin point, to the recognition of themselves as pure Creation. Those who were to assume a leadership role in their society were often the recipients. After this rite of passage, their destiny was to become a conduit of Life Itself, allowing the wisdom of Source to awaken, informing their every decision as leader or wisdom-keeper of their people.

This ceremony, in its fullness, would be impossible to replicate today. Nor would it be appropriate for our modern minds and sensibilities. The wisdom of this Pathway, however, is open to all of us.

Thanks to Kahu's willingness to share this deep and powerful work, we are able to step into the potent discovery of Creation Itself inside of ourselves, restoring our communion with Life on all levels, from the molecular to the divine.

I arrived at my first training with Kahu expecting to deepen my practice of what I knew as Lomi Lomi, and quickly found myself bewildered. Our days were filled largely with cleaning the toilet, setting the table, washing the dishes and sweeping the lanai, interspersed with a few movement practices, some taught by Kahu's wife, Ho'okahi. She directed us from activity to activity with strict standards as to how everything should be done. Kahu appeared from time to time, speaking very little, and saying little about what I had come to hear. After about three days I wondered what I was doing there.

His presence was like a force of nature. It felt as if he could see right through me, hear every thought, sense every flaw in me. I had never met such an individual. The atmosphere brought me to an acute attention of everything going on inside of me. In addition to every thought, I had a heightened awareness of the way I moved, of sensations, rhythm, taste, and sound. At the same time, I realized that I was trying really hard to get everything "right" to win Kahu's approval, a seemingly impossible task. My negative self-talk became louder and more persistent than it had ever been. No matter what I did, I was sure it wasn't acceptable.

Every time Kahu looked at me, I was convinced it was a look of disapproval. The rest of the time I felt ignored. I was positive he considered me a lost cause. The harder I tried to get it right, the louder these internal voices became.

Little by little I began to settle into the environment, or probably more accurately, into myself. It was as if the walls themselves began to change. Magically, what had felt like cramped bunk bed accommodations suddenly seemed spacious. The house we were staying in changed from dank and dark to bright and welcoming. My internal turbulence seemed to become increasingly quiet.

As part of the training, we were taught a repetitive dance-like movement meditation called Ka'alele 'au, or Flying. This movement has every part of the body moving in the shape of infinity, the figure eight. The head, torso, arms, hips, legs, and feet were all meant to move in one harmonious, connected, infinite wave. The seemingly simple movements bewildered my body and confused my brain. I was constantly on the wrong leg, stepping in the wrong direction, or looking the wrong way.

In the rare moments when I could feel some harmony begin to emerge, I became busy trying to create "perfect lines" with my arms and legs as I was taught to do as a dancer. My efforts only threw me out of rhythm, and became exhausting.

One day the class was set to Flying in the living room facing the kitchen door, above which was a large wall clock. After giving us instructions not to stop, Kahu and Ho'okahi promptly left the room. Watching the clock, which was right in front of me, I focused on the seconds ticking by, then the minutes. It was excruciating. I had never felt a minute last so long. About ten minutes later, my arms already beginning to tire, I heard Kahu's truck start up. Looking through a space in the blinds, we watched as he and his wife drove away.

A wave of panic swept through the room. Unless they returned right away, our hopes of stopping anytime soon were dashed.

Four and a half hours later, the truck pulled into the driveway. Only one person in the class had stopped. The rest of us had kept going through an indescribable spectrum of thought, emotion, sensation, imagery, memory, color, and shape. Somehow we hadn't stopped despite arms that felt as heavy as tree trunks and legs that had turned to rubber. My feelings ranged from utter despair to indescribable joy, touching everything in between.

Pain and joy that seemed to have no origin point cascaded through me. Other images and feelings were more specific. I cried at the memory of my mother's disappointment in me, and my father's emotional distance. A long blank space arose in which I appeared to have no thoughts or emotions at all. Finally, the image of a simple daisy I had stopped to admire the day before flooded my system. The tiny daisy revealed itself as a massive, powerfully loving Being. I felt a pure and all-encompassing love flow through me. I cried from the overwhelming feeling of being completely loved. I cried because I felt I didn't deserve it. I cried because I couldn't believe that Life, through the eyes of this tiny Being, saw me, remembered me and came to support me when I needed it most. From that point on, an indescribable joy arose. My arms and legs became light and strong. The flying became effortless, as if it were happening all by itself. A pure energy emerged in my body. I was ready to fly forever.

When Kahu finally had us stop, we stood still with our eyes closed for a time. My body was buzzing on the inside, from the skin to deep inside the bones, all vibrating, almost audibly humming. Energy was surging through me that I had never experienced before. I felt like most of my brain was missing and in its place was endless motion and utter stillness at the same time.

A few days later, sharing some of my experience with his wife Ho'okahi, I asked, "Where did all of this energy come from? Are these the ancestors or the lineage of the work? What I felt could not possibly be only me!" She replied, "Oh yes it could. There is more in you than you can know. All of it was you."

That was my first experience of "stepping across the line" – going beyond what I thought was possible – and entering a world beyond my imagination. If there is anything consistent that I have noticed on this Pathway, it is that there is always an invitation to step into the unknown. The thresholds of new horizons seem to appear when I least expect them, and often it feels as if I am leaving everything behind.

"Finally, you understand yourself to be the walking, breathing Truth. "
— Kahu Abraham Kawai'i

INTEGRATION EXERCISE • STEPPING ACROSS THE LINE

To experience an opening to the awareness alive in your body, practice this Integration on page 102 that will allow you to begin to awaken and strengthen your ability to listen to the miracle of the body's consciousness. This is an infinite door leading to a direct experience of your own Spirit, awake in the body

CHAPTER 2
THE BODY IS ALIVE

UNBOUND

High
Clear
Far away
and now closer,
the sound of my foot
stepping into a clear stream.
My eyes on the horizon
of wild things,
The taste in my mouth,
Freedom.
Unbuckling the harness from my heart,
I gallop
and sing
songs before unheard,
keeping rhythm with the cold, clear water,
and the night sky
full of stars.

—J. Mountain (2015)

We in the modern world forget that we are made of magic, meaning that which we do not fully understand. We each are born out of the mystical meeting of an egg and sperm. From the moment of conception, our developing life is governed by a Mystery that allows our cells to replicate, specialize and form into an unfathomably complex organism. We are born with this mysterious force of Life which will pour through us endlessly until the moment we die. Without our knowledge or intention, our heart will beat, oxygen will be delivered to every cell, over 75,000 enzymes will be secreted at the exact times and in the exact amounts they are needed, our food will be digested, our eyes will be lubricated and if we live to the age of 80, we will likely have taken over 600 million automatic breaths.

The ancient Hawaiians believed that the body was the keeper of Universal truths. Instead of going up and out to God and the Angels, they would go deeper into the cells of the body to find answers to the same questions humans have asked throughout the ages: "Who am I?" "What or who is God?" "What is the meaning of life?" Much more than a "machine" requiring the right food, rest, and exercise, the body, according to Ancient Wisdom, is a living, breathing, light-filled intelligence far beyond the conscious mind.

For those of us raised in Western traditions, it can be challenging to think that this same body of ours, which we may have been taught to view, at best, as an obstacle to be overcome, holds the very keys to our spiritual search. Throughout the ages, we have been taught that the Sacred is out of our reach, far above the impurity of the body: pristine, elevated, pure and most importantly, connected with an ethereal and disembodied God.

What if just the opposite is true? What if the Sacred is operating in and through everything, including our own bodies, minds and emotions? What if everything is sacred just because it exists? What if each of us is born of the Sacred, in Original Innocence rather than Original Sin? How would this recognition change how we navigate and experience our lives? We may find ourselves in a new matrix of understanding. In other words, rather than darkness and light, sacred and profane, we might experience the energy of motion or stuckness, inspiration or lack of choice, expansion or contraction, stillness or flow.

Ancient Wisdom, guides us back to our natural origins, filled with the same life force as the nature that surrounds us. Deep below our conscious perceptions of who we are is the same Life that allows an acorn to grow into a giant oak tree and is right now birthing countless stars. The same material found in all of Life is found in our bodies. As human beings, we share DNA with all life on the planet. As carbon-based beings, our cells contain remnants of exploding stars. In fact, astrophysicists have concluded that about 93% of the mass in our bodies is stardust. Within that mass, however, 99.9999% of it is space. Indigenous peoples have known this for thousands of years. The Ancients forged pathways to the space within. Their wisdom teaches us that this innate force, permeating every cell of our bodies, is awake and alive with consciousness.

Regardless of the outer trappings of our modern world, and our tendency to live from our conceptual minds, our deep interrelationship with all of Life has not changed. Although we may identify with who we believe ourselves to be, the truth is, we are simply Creation in motion.

When we consider just what has occurred in our bodies in the past twenty-four hours, without our conscious participation, we might realize that even our most brilliant thoughts are tiny in comparison. Since yesterday, the Life of your body has shed and replaced approximately 1.5 million skin cells, renewed 30% of your stomach lining, and pumped up to 2,000 gallons of blood through your heart feeding approximately 100,000 miles of blood vessels – a distance covering four times around the circumference of the Earth. Clearly, we are animated by a wise universal intelligence that is beyond our comprehension.

Our modern worldview tends to glorify the brain as the seat of our intelligence and orchestrator of all bodily systems. It is perhaps even where we in the West believe consciousness lies.

When we look at the Earth, we might notice that there is no central control center regulating ocean currents or wind velocity. There is no central command telling animals how to behave, when to migrate or hibernate. Each aspect of this world is simply moving as Life Itself. Though there may be a scientific explanation as to why some animals migrate and hibernate, science still has not uncovered a central "brain" of the Earth, let alone the Universe. Animals, microbes, plants, winds, clouds, planets, stars, and bodies of water are simply moving in the deep harmony of Creation.

Similarly, the brain may not actually be the absolute master of the body. Science has discovered that the heart has its own "brain", meaning that the heart can make its own decisions that may conflict with directives from the central nervous system. Scientists then discovered that the intestinal tract has its own brain, with the same independent functioning as the heart.

If the Ancients are right, science will eventually discover that every cell has its own brain. Perhaps we are not yet at the point where we can imagine that we comprise 100 trillion independent beings choosing harmony and cooperation resulting in a united and seamless whole. But according to Ancient Wisdom, this is exactly what we are.

Indigenous worldview guides us to uproot our hierarchical vision of the natural world as well as our own bodies. It is guiding us toward inhabiting ourselves as whole beings. As we begin to pay attention to the Life of our Cellular Being, it begins to respond. We are met by Life and rather than trying to control it, we begin moving in cooperation with this living force. We begin to hear its unique voice, to witness its unfolding, guiding us toward more well-being than we can imagine.

Developing a relationship with my Cellular Being has been much more than an idea. As I was able to shift my perception of my body from a concept to a vast collection of living beings, my body, in many ways, has responded with a heightened cooperation that enhances the health, vitality, and awareness of my entire system.

A few years ago, concerned about a possible infection, I asked my dentist if he would remove a tooth that had undergone a root canal. He examined my mouth and agreed. "Please be aware," he said, "that your tooth is firmly embedded in your gum and your gums are quite strong. It is likely that this tooth will be unable to come out in one piece and will probably break. After this, I'll have to dig the rest of the tooth out of your gum. Be prepared for about a two-hour procedure." I listened and agreed to go ahead.

As I waited for the appointment, I spent time with that tooth, addressing it as a conscious being and letting it know what was about to happen. I listened, without interpretation, as its sensations, temperature and texture undulated. A name even popped out of the listening: Chester. As the day of the extraction arrived, I felt a great deal of calm in my mouth and in my system. Chester and I were ready.

I should mention that I have the most wonderful holistic dentist. He listens attentively and makes a point of telling his clients exactly what he's doing in each moment. Before he began the procedure, I told him I had a special and rather strange request. I relayed briefly that I was working with a belief system in which each part of our body is alive and conscious. "So, while you are working with my tooth," I continued, "would you mind addressing it directly and asking for its cooperation?" I stopped short of telling him that my tooth had a name. My dentist smiled, finding my request amusing, but agreed.

As he began the procedure, he started to give me the usual play-by-play description of each aspect of the work. It was, as always, reassuring to know what exactly was happening. At one point, he was silent for a long time. Just when I was beginning to wonder what was going on, he said, "I'm talking to your tooth."

About two minutes later, it was out. The entire procedure took half an hour as the tooth came out easily and in one piece. I still have Chester in a little plastic envelope and feel so grateful to him for his cooperation.

If this sounds like a description through the eyes of a child, in a way, it is. As young children we knew that there was Life in everything, whether it was supposed to be alive or not. To our adult minds, this is "nonsense". We are taught to set aside infinite possibility in favor of logic. Unfortunately, this means we abandon a relationship with the magnificent Life inside of us. We lose the ability to perceive the body as the home of Spirit, of infinite energy, possibility, and living wisdom. In a sense, returning to a living relationship with the body is like coming back to the eyes of a child, to the endless discovery and wonder this brings.

Opening to our cellular consciousness means that we begin to question the belief that the Divine is outside of us. Ancient Wisdom tells us that we are made of it. Wherever we are, and whatever we are doing, the Infinite inside of us is also there, available to be met. Allowing ourselves to once again see through the eyes of our childhood innocence reveals each brand new moment of discovery, in communion with the Divine.

In this ancient paradigm, we have the opportunity to rejoin an infinite dance, beyond our imagination, unfolding within us. In every moment, we touch and are being touched by, the Sacred.

"We are made of Beings within Beings, Spheres within Spheres, Lives within Lives, Worlds within Worlds, Universes within Universes."
— Kahu Abraham Kawai'i

🔥 INTEGRATION EXERCISE • THE BODY IS ALIVE

After years, or even decades of familiarity with our limited concept of the body, It can be challenging to see it in a new way. Practice the Integration Exercise on page 104 to ignite new possibilities.

CHAPTER 3
ʻOHANA NUI • THE GREAT FAMILY

THE REMEMBERING

We are Mauna Kea
We are Haleakalā
We are the desert of Qumran
We are the Amazon
We are the River Lee
We are the Blue Mountains
We are the Arctic Sea
We are the Tundra

We are the breath of the Wind
The Sparkling Sea
We are the Ripened Fruit
And the Fertile Soil
We are the Seed, the Blossoming,
and the Harvest

We are the rhythm of the Earth as it spins
We are the Water as it falls from the sky
We are the shining Stars
The Remembering,
and The Light in each other's eyes.

—J. Mountain (2015)

During my very first training, I was initially flooded with the memory of home. Not the home of my childhood or my home country, but a long-forgotten place where I knew I belonged. Walking through rolling wooded hillsides full of wildlife, I felt my body relax. As I walked and listened, my breath deepened, and a new space opened inside.

I recognized the hills, trees and all the abundant life around me as I would long-lost friends or relatives. The inflated balloon of my personal thoughts, ideas, intentions, and emotions became insignificant in the presence of the vast, loud resonance of Life Itself. It was so massive and all pervasive, I wondered how I could possibly have blocked it out until now.

I became hyperaware of my surroundings, mostly earth, trees, sun, sky, clouds, and birds. The natural world became alive with constant movement, sound, and vitality I had never experienced before. The trees seemed to be ablaze with energy, life force, and even personality. I felt like I was walking amongst close friends, each step a whole conversation with the ground beneath my feet.

One afternoon, our teacher, Patrick, gave us a break after lunch. We were to be back in the workshop space at 3p.m. I decided to go for a walk in the woods and came upon a tree which had fallen, providing a perfect bench. I sat gazing out onto a lush valley with rolling hills in the distance. Before long, I was transported into what felt like an energetic soup of earth, trees, sky, wind, sun, and my own breath. Although new to my awareness, the sensations were undeniably familiar to my body. More than connectedness, this rhythmic sameness with all that surrounded me felt like my natural state, alive underneath the distractions of my mind. After a while I was joined by four small birds that landed exactly together on a low-hanging branch a few feet in front of my face. As soon as they landed, we were instantly in communication, although I couldn't hope to describe how. We were just part of one another. Each tiny movement they made felt like a movement inside of me. At the time, it was not remarkable, but felt completely natural. Sometime later, the bird family flew off exactly together, just as they had arrived. I knew, without a doubt, it was time to return. I found myself back in the workshop space at ten minutes past three. Coming in the door with me was our teacher, ready to start the afternoon session.

Although I didn't know the concept at the time, it was my first experience of 'Ohana Nui (The Great Family.)

In Ancient Hawaiian culture, 'Ohana, or Family is a foundation of every aspect of life. Hawaiian creation stories speak of Papa, Earth Mother and Wākea, Sky Father. They recognize the Kalo (Taro plant) as their first blood relative and every plant and type of rain as having their own unique qualities of contribution to the 'Ohana Nui.

'Ohana includes the immediate family, the greater community, plants, animals, ocean, earth, sky, sun, stars, and elements. Ancient peoples experienced the same Spirit in all forms of life. Seeing all that surrounds us as family reveals a nourishing depth of connection with the natural world and fosters unity in our consciousness. Every member of this 'Ohana is welcome as brother, sister, mother, father, and child, all originating from the same Creation that allows each of us to be alive.

The continuous ebb and flow of each aspect of Creation generates balance, abundance, and well-being among all the aspects. We all live in an intricate, symbiotic relationship with everything that exists. What begins on the mountaintop, ends up in the sea. What begins in the oceans and rivers ends up in the clouds to pour down as nourishment for the plants and animals.

Humankind, being a part of this Great Family, is also a part of this intrinsic balance. Our role, as the ancients knew, is to abide in harmony with the rest of the 'Ohana and to care for them.

To understand the Indigenous worldview, it might be helpful to take note of the language Indigenous people use to describe their place in the world. Western mind speaks about our "connection with nature". Indigenous mind speaks of themselves *as* nature, or as a relative of nature. There is no space between the Indigenous idea of the natural world, and themselves. Indigenous mind is able to perceive its place in the cosmology of all of Life, recognizing that the very same Spirit animates all being. All interactions with the natural world become a loving conversation. Indigenous people have a passion for caring for the land, water, and creatures not because of what they can gain, but because they are inseparable.

Our modern evolution, however, has taken us far from fulfilling our original place as a part of the Earth. Instead, we imagine humans to be superior and therefore destined to be in control. We live in an adopted hierarchy of greater beings in charge of lesser beings. Ironically, the emerging new paradigm is being remembered from our ancient past. We, as a species, are coming face-to-face with the consequences of our misperceptions. We have acted on a belief that is simply not true – that we are separate and even superior to nature. We have operated in isolation on so many levels. Now, as the consequences of our misperceptions become manifest, we are beginning to experience the interconnectedness of all being.

In our panic, our solution is to rush to fix our errors: decrease carbon emissions, plant millions of trees, ban certain plastics, mount massive efforts to clean the oceans. Yet we are still operating from a sense of separation, acting out of fear for our own existence.

Coming back to our original, Indigenous sensibilities brings us to a restoration of our true relationship with the nature around us. It brings us back to our place in the family of all of Life. If we can restore our perceptions to meet the Earth as our Mother and each plant and animal as a relative, we can recover "right relationship" with our precious Earth. We will be acting because we care about our relatives, not because we are afraid for our lives. We will care for the Earth because we will recognize her as part of who we are. This is 'Ohana: cultivating relationships that are founded in connection, reciprocity, and love.

On the pathway of Ke Ala Hōkū, this foundational principle is expanded to include our internal world. What if we could see every facet of who we are and what we experience as Family? Ancient Wisdom tells us that every aspect of our cellular being as well as all of our sensations, emotions, memories, thoughts, beliefs, perceptions, hopes, and dreams are all members of our internal family. Coming into a familial relationship with every part of us opens up new communication, greater energy flow, and a pathway back to our own wholeness.

For centuries, we in the Western world have been fed a worldview that is intrinsically divided. We are relentlessly programmed to believe in the polarities of good versus bad, right versus wrong and light versus dark. Over time, what we have placed into each category has largely been dictated to us by religion and the changing moral landscape of each era and culture. As a result, our perceptions are imperceptibly colored by the division between right and wrong. Even below our conscious awareness, most of what we perceive in the world around us automatically falls into one category or the other.

More importantly, however, how we perceive ourselves is caught in this same divisive paradigm. Our thoughts, emotions and behaviors are split between concepts of good and bad. We are taught that parts of ourselves are to be embraced, encouraged, and loved and that other parts are to be overcome, discarded, rejected, or even killed.

Regardless of the doctrine of an all-loving God found in most religions, we are taught that parts of ourselves are simply unacceptable in the eyes of the Divine. Our internal world becomes a fractured one. We spend a tremendous amount of energy trying to get rid of what we consider to be bad about ourselves while striving to be good. For some of us, the stakes are very high, our struggle perhaps culminating in a fate with only two choices: heaven or hell.

Knowing themselves to be the same substance and life as the Earth, the Ancients looked to nature to understand and navigate their internal world. They observed that every aspect of nature is accepted for its unique place and contribution to the whole. There is no part of the Earth that is considered bad or wrong. The desert, tundra, grassland, volcano, and even hurricane are each fulfilling a unique function on Earth. Everything is deeply interconnected. Everything belongs, everything is 'Ohana.

The same is true inside of us. In the ancient world view, beyond the concept of good and bad lies the reality of Unity – the recognition that every emotion, event, thought, or behavior that has arisen in our lives is an undeniable part of who we are. We cannot delete them by pretending they never occurred.

Our task is to welcome these parts of ourselves back into the family. As we begin to extend our acceptance toward everything inside of us, and reunite our internal 'Ohana, we begin to meet parts of ourselves that have been separated, divorced, feared, estranged, entombed or banished. We begin the journey of welcoming and accepting all members of our Internal 'Ohana and begin the journey back toward our original, unified being. We recognize that every aspect of who we are is made of the same foundation of Life that both surrounds and inhabits us.

There is a vast amount of new information, connection and experience revealed in every moment if we are able to exhume ourselves from the tomb of repetitive thinking, and inhabit a world where the family of Life is constantly in deep communication with us.

Indigenous Mind begins with the knowing that we exist as Life, in the midst of Life, and that all of Life is our Family. There is great humility in taking our rightful place. Our old paradigm of being the ones in charge, the ones who know best, the ones who are the most powerful, is over. It has proven itself not only to be unsustainable, but simply not true. As a result, we find ourselves in a crisis of survival woven by our old, misguided doctrines and beliefs.

The consequences of our actions are serving as a bright beacon, calling us back home to live in harmony with the rest of our 'Ohana Nui. We are being called to listen to the resonance of Life inside of ourselves and all around us. In doing so, we will come into harmony with a greater reality than the separation created through our limited minds. We will contribute to the thriving of all living beings, rather than being the destroyers. We will restore our right relationship with ourselves, each other, and the Earth. We will ourselves become the embodiment of a New Paradigm.

"The beauty of the trees, the softness of the air, the fragrance of the grass, they speak to me. The summit of the mountain, the thunder of the sky, the rhythm of the sea, speaks to me. The faintness of the stars, the freshness of the morning, the dewdrop on the flower, speaks to me. The strength of the fire, the taste of the salmon, the trail of the sun, and the life that never goes away, they speak to me. And my heart soars. "

— Chief Dan George

INTEGRATION EXERCISE • 'OHANA NUI

This experiential exercise on page 106 will open new pathways to closer relationship with the Life inside and around us, igniting our cellular memory of 'Ohana Nui.

Chapter 4
INTERNAL NAVIGATION

WAVES WITHIN WAVES

Tonight, I swam into the depths
Of an Ocean so vast,
I could not imagine it.

Endless motion danced me.
The rhythm of waves within waves
Carried me beyond time,
And lifted me,
Drifted me,
Inside out.

Tonight, I swam in golden light
And in letting go.

— J. Mountain (2018)

The now-rare book, *Children of the Night Rainbow,* gives a beautiful recounting of 'Ohana stories passed down from Kailii'ohe Kamae'ekua of Kamalo, Moloka'i by authors Pali Jae Lee and Koko Willis. One of its captivating stories relays that each human is born with a perfect bowl of light. "If he tends his Light, it will grow in strength and he can do all things – swim with the shark, fly with the birds, know and understand all things."

When I first read this story, my understanding was that as life unfolds, our experiences of hurt, betrayal, injustice, fear, and so on, are like stones that get placed in the bowl, covering much of our precious light. Our job in life is to turn over the bowl, letting all the stones fall out, so we may shine fully again with our original light. However, as I re-read this wise book, I realize that it actually says that if we "become envious or jealous, [we] drop a stone into [our] Bowl of Light and some of the Light goes out."

Based on my original understanding, for a long time I had been trying to turn over my bowl. Yet as I navigated on this pathway, I found it impossible to empty my bowl and to let the stones fall out. The simple reason was that every stone, as I understood it – every hurt, pain, disappointment, trauma and tragedy – could not be undone. What I found instead was an opportunity to remember and to cultivate this original light, allowing the stones to become its fuel. Though my original misunderstanding took me down a slightly different path, I came to realize that our light can become even brighter because of what we have been through.

How do we cultivate our essential Light so that every situation we face contributes to our forward motion?

Both quantum physicists and ancient wisdom teachers tell us that everything in the known Universe begins and ends with frequency. Quantum Physics often leads us to this in the description of matter. Everything that seems solid, according to quantum field research, is actually a compilation of vibrating particles that produce various frequencies.

Ancient Wisdom goes further, identifying circumstances, emotions, thoughts and actions also as manifestations of frequency. All of who we are – how we perceive, speak, and act – produces specific vibrations. How we relate to ourselves, how we relate to others, how we perceive our bodies and the world around us, all create frequency. Our conscious and unconscious habits and beliefs all create frequency. These vibrations combined create what I call our "essential resonance".

Each frequency, including every perception, emotion, thought, and action, are members of our internal 'Ohana.

How we meet and metabolize what arises in both our inner and outer worlds will result in enhancing our essential resonance or in depleting it. For example, if I tend to meet the outer world with opposition, blaming others for my discontent, my energy will be drained in the fight to be right.

This Indigenous paradigm offers us a new way of navigating in Natural Order. It guides us to recognize that everything we feel belongs to us. As we embrace whatever is arising, and welcome it back into the family, we reunite our system. Each difficult emotion, memory or situation can find its way home.

Just like family systems in nature, there are parents and children in our internal world. Kahu referred to our undulating emotions and reactions as the children of our internal 'Ohana. Just like a child, each has its own, usually very focused point of view and each is fully consumed with the energy of the moment. Anger can only feel anger. Shame only wants to hide. Depression can't see the light at the end of the tunnel, and so on. Our default reactions, consistent or habitual thought patterns, and emotional patterns would all be considered children of our internal 'Ohana.

There is one member of our internal family, however, that holds an expansive viewpoint, one who can listen to the distress of all the children in pure acceptance. Kahu called this being "The Head of our Household". The Head of our Household, like a loving mother-father combination, provides the foundation, structure, support, nurturance, and love in the home, in the archetypal sense. It is the one who can embrace the whole family, listen to everyone, and then ultimately take the actions that enhance the well-being of all.

Just like a wise parent, the Head of our Household can bring each child closer, and in a loving embrace, listen to the grief, anger, fear, resistance, pain, or insecurity that child may be feeling. As each is given the space to be seen and heard, the mana (energy) of these hurt parts of ourselves has an opportunity to unfold in our system. Energy that was held, repressed, bound up in conflict or seemingly banished becomes free to contribute to our forward motion in life, rather than hold us back.

If, instead, we allow ourselves to be ruled by each child as its needs arise, we will likely live a tumultuous life. To have the children sit at the head of the dinner table and decide what the family will have for dinner each night would be unwise. As in a human family, children are not meant to be in charge. They do not have sufficient perspective to govern and direct the actions of the family as a whole. They are to be loved and guided as they grow.

No matter how much we try to suppress difficult emotions or events in our lives, the truth remains that they are part of who we are and what we have experienced. No matter what has triggered them, they belong to us. The more we try to deny this simple fact by pushing them away, burying, or banishing them from our awareness, the more they will persist. In an effort to be acknowledged, they will often speak louder and louder in a variety of ways.

For example, if I am in the habit of pushing down my inner child of frustration or anger, that energy will keep building inside of me with no outlet, getting stronger and stronger. One day, a very simple thing may happen – perhaps someone cuts me off in traffic – and suddenly I am exploding with an anger that is out of proportion to the situation. It's as if a member of your family comes to your front door for a family gathering and knocks. If you don't let them in they will knock louder. If they get no response, they will start pounding on the door and eventually break it down altogether. This seems like a harsh analogy, but it is our internal family's cry for recognition. All parts of us are wanting to be included in our experience. None of our internal children want to be told that they do not deserve to belong. Even if we would rather not accept their presence, the truth is that they are indeed each an inseparable part of who we are.

Our learned response to difficult or contentious parts of ourselves is often to label them as "bad" and do our best to make them go away. We consciously and unconsciously deny, supress, ignore, and even psychoanalyze aspects of ourselves that we believe should not be there.

Counterintuitvely to our modern minds, Ancient Wisdom guides us not only to listen to these unwanted energies, but to bring them closer. This can be a frightening proposition when we are afraid that they are more powerful than we are. However if we can cultivate an awareness of our Head of Household, we come into contact with a wise power within that allows a great embrace of even our worst fears and traumas. Resting in this expansive space, we can ask our internal 'ohana to tell us more about themselves. We can listen without fear, knowing that they are simply one of our inner children crying out. When we are able to let the hurt and banished internal family members finally speak, we allow old, stagnant energy to become free. No longer trapped in the pain of isolation, they are transmuted into contributing members of our internal family – energy that assists us in moving forward in life. As we adopt this approach to our inner world, we find ourselves resting in an internal environment of compassion for the very parts of ourselves we may have previously rejected.

Before we can embrace the children of our internal 'Ohana, however, we must recognize them as our own. Acknowledging them and aligning our awareness with the wide perspective of Head of Household, we can shift from feeling like a victim to embodying the alchemy of acceptance and the embrace of Aloha (unconditional love).

In our modern Western culture, the opinions of others as well as the circumstances of our lives are usually deemed the cause of our internal state of being. When everything is great, and life is the way we want it, we are happy. When circumstances change, and things are no longer matching what we want, we may become angry, sad, frustrated or depressed. The physiological and psychological truth, however, is that no matter what the outer circumstance, whatever emotion rises inside of us is energy of our own making. This is energy we have generated in our own system.

If we are brave enough to welcome our inner children, and acknowledge them as beings of our own creation, we can begin to reclaim the power over our own well-being that we have given away to others.

This Pathway of internal navigation is not asking us to blame ourselves for our outer circumstances. It is simply asking us to recognize that our response belongs to us. All aspects of who we are, are alive, awake, and vibrating as living frequencies. We respond in the ways we do, not because of the external world, but because one of those often unresolved parts of ourselves has dominated our perspective in the moment.

As we embrace those members of our Internal 'Ohana that are deeply hurt, we set foot on the path to reuniting ourselves at the core. Most importantly, we claim responsibility for our internal world. Our joy, freedom, and intrinsic safety become an inside job. We restore a wholeness that cannot be shaken by outer events.

If one of the children of the family takes over, however, chaos can ensure. Our bandwidth of possibility narrows to a single emotion or belief. This is the time when we can lose control, lash out, shut down, or implode inward. If you remember any time in your life where you "lost it", you may discover that there was a certain emotion or belief that completely dominated your perspective like the phenomenon of 'seeing red' which describes someone utterly consumed by anger.

Navigating from the broad perspective of The Head of our Household offers us the possibility of acting from choice, in the interest of our well-being and the well-being of all that surrounds us. A much wider spectrum of possibilities can be seen, felt, and heard. Each member of our inner family can ultimately be included to allow a decision that benefits our Internal 'Ohana as a whole. Coming from this more expansive place, without our automatic tendency to blame outer circumstances, we may discover a more harmonious response from others.

There is an opportunity in every moment, to meet, embrace, and free more of ourselves. We can learn to rest in the wider space of compassion that is the Head of our Household, and navigate life from this place instead of from the limited view of one of our internal children. As we cultivate the willingness to meet the less loved or frightening parts ourselves, we become a vehicle for our own transformation, turning rejection into loving embrace and pain into resilience.

Restoring the Natural Order of our Internal 'Ohana allows us to meet each living moment as it is. Instead of pushing difficult feelings down or away, this internal navigation gives us a way to accept them. We move from a fractured inner world, toward wholeness.

Ancient Wisdom guides us to the understanding that below our superficial awareness, we are living in the vast reciprocal generosity of 'Ohana Nui – The Great Family within.

"As the Kahuna Philosophy stands, the key factor in personal or self-development is to understand that all that you are – your thoughts, your actions, your fears, your anger, your griefs, your judgments, your decisions, your happiness, your greatness, your intelligence – are all 'Members of Your Family'. Once born they remain in your 'Space of Existence' with varying degrees and percentages of activity for the remainder of your life and beyond."
—Kahu Abraham Kawai'i

INTEGRATION EXERCISE · INTERNAL NAVIGATION

This powerful exercise on page 107 will allow you to meet your Internal Family, opening new avenues of energy and presence in your inner world.

Chapter 5
OUR PERCEPTIVE FIELD

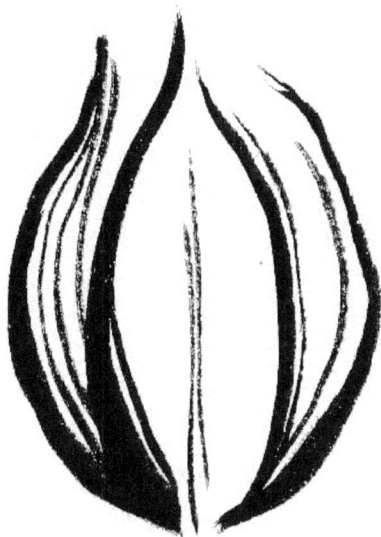

HANA

Waking up before dawn to a million crickets
Black sky, Bright stars
Stillness.
I gather my few things in an old string bag
And start up the pathway of illumination
The pathway lined with Kukui.
As I step, I feel the earth breathe, lifting my feet on every inhale.
Looking up into the tree tops, I notice the sky is now barely glowing.
My vision feels like it is deep inside my head, and somehow in the trees at the same time.
I walk dumbfounded that my regular sight has disappeared,
And in its place this kind of multi-sourced seeing.
Disoriented and intrigued, I walk,
feeling the crunch of stone on the soles of my feet,
Not sure where "I" am, or am not.
Listening to my vision,
Listening to the forest.
I say a quick prayer, in case anyone is listening,
As I speak, a pitter patter of leaves erupts in the forest right beside me,
A murmuring.
Individual leaves shudder and flap wildly, though most of the trees are still.
A sprinkle of rain is the only logical explanation I can come up with.
I look up – no clouds, no breeze
Just the forest, wide awake and listening.
We are in open communion with each other.
We are the breathing green, the waking light, the altered gaze, the damp morning air,
The stone and dirt meeting feet.
We have gazed into each others eyes, this morning and I,
Seeing will never be the same again.

—J. Mountain (2014)

"The work is every moment of your life."

Kahu's words rang through my head that entire first training. There to learn a form of bodywork, I had no clue what he was talking about. My mind was moving in the compartmentalized ways of my schooling. If the work was every moment of my life, then he couldn't be talking about the bodywork. I struggled with the concept and let it go many times. It has taken years to discover this elusive "work", and the years of deepening continue.

Although it persistently feels like I am still just scratching the surface, I recognize the work now as a way of being. On one level, it is the journey of being more and more willing to step out of my habitual way of perceiving. This leaves me, over and over again, in the unknown. Learning to listen deeply makes this void a crucible of discovery rather than a frightening place. I am hearing, seeing, and feeling depths of perception previously hidden. No longer are things just as I have known them to be; they are full of the multiple dimensions, colors, sounds, smells, impressions, rhythms, and textures of Life in motion. Aspects previously just beyond my gaze reveal themselves, allowing me to perceive more possibilities than my preconceived notions would allow. Living in a state of wonder, nothing is mundane.

It is this phenomenal process of Life meeting Life that ignites my journey and takes me to each new threshold of discovery.

Kahu, used to say, "Perception is everything." Indeed, nothing shapes our reality more than the way we perceive. Our responses to life are formed, not so much by what happens, as by our interpretation. The way we see and respond to life is created through a complex history of genetic, familial, social, cultural, and religious programming. From the time we are born, our choices, behaviors and responses are given to us. In the background of this programming is the core of what keeps these learned behaviors in place. It is the ground of not what we see, but the very way we perceive it.

We in the West have learned to understand everything through classification and compartmentalization. We separate the human body into cells, fluids, tissues, organs and organ systems. We form our concepts about others based on wealth or poverty, able-bodied or disabled, young or old, intelligent or mentally impaired. We separate through culture, ethnicity, gender and sexual orientation. We break down the natural world particle by particle, species by species, setting ourselves apart, the crown jewel of our intelligence making us "superior to Nature". We are locked in a perception of separation, while the reality that we are intrinsically whole beings birthed by Earth herself is lost to millennia of conditioning.

In the midst of the multiple ways we can be influenced, we unconsciously learn the mechanism of perception itself. We come to embody a way of digesting the world, based on a combination of our belief systems and science, that never comes into question. Once we can quantify, measure and label something, we have a certified, proven fact. Quantifying and proving in the matrix of our compartmentalized perception has become the basis of our belief. How we perceive is so natural to us, there seems to be no other possibility.

While there is nothing wrong with breaking down and examining the components of things, the Western Mind is seemingly frozen in this paradigm. It has become our predominant way of perceiving. How do we return to natural perception? Ancient Wisdom asks us to step beyond the limitations of the mind and into the realm of the unknown.

Just below the superficial level of our conscious awareness, and even below the knowledge base of our minds, our entire body is actually experiencing each moment of our lives. Our bodies inhabit each living present moment, experiencing the interrelationship of sounds, smells, sensations, vibrations, rhythms, colors, shapes, images, and motion. No matter what our thoughts are or what we know or believe, every second of our lives, our whole body is immersed in the dynamic undulations of Life. Regardless of how much we superimpose our learned thoughts, opinions, and beliefs, we are in actuality receiving the world through a field of perception that includes our entire system.

This ancient pathway guides us to return to the living being of each present moment, rather than our interpretations of what is here now. We can expand the limitations of our current perceptions, by listening through the vast spectrum of the body. We can listen with our entire perceptive field. Listening from this deeply connected place, we are able to perceive a multidimensional reality far beyond the programming of divisiveness.

The undeniable truth is that, as you read this, your heart is beating, your lungs are delivering oxygen carried by your arteries to every cell, nerves are firing, cells throughout are dying and being replaced, and somewhere inside of you, your emotions, memories, hopes, and dreams are in motion. Most of this is ignored because it lies below the radar of our immediate attention, but the truth is that every iota of you is here now, in a living relationship with this moment. From your baby toe to the saliva in your mouth – all of you is generating, perceiving and participating as the consciousness of Life Itself.

Science tells us that our conscious mind is able to process at a rate of approximately 40 bits of information per second while our subconscious mind processes at approximately 40 million bits of information per second. Our senses alone collect 11 million bits of information per second from the environment. In the last five seconds, 200 million bits of information were received and managed by your subconscious throughout the body, the vast majority of it below the level of your awareness.

This means that we are receiving multiple depths of information in any given moment. While our minds are steadily focused on wherever our attention is, our body is receiving an immeasurable amount of multi-dimensional sounds, smells, tastes, sensations, rhythms, and temperatures. Our body is, in fact, the primary receiver of most of what we experience.

The recognition that everything we can perceive inhabits multiple depths of being is perfectly expressed by the Hawaiian word, *Kaona*. *Kaona* was originally used in the interpretation of language, often chant, poetry, or sacred teachings. Its literal translation is "hidden meaning", referring to layers of insight into the words, imagery, or concepts. The closest idea to this in English is "allegory", or "symbolic representation" found in literature.

For example, a chant about the beauty of a particular flower budding and then coming to blossom, may be understood as just that – an admiration for this being and all the beauty it brings to the world. A deeper kaona of the chant may refer to a student gathering knowledge from her teacher and then blossoming with the support of that path. Another may tell of a woman becoming pregnant and blossoming into birth. Yet another might perceive the connection of Life Itself in all that is constantly blossoming into beauty, new Life and new forms of existence. Depending on the context in which it is presented, many levels of meaning may be conveyed to those who are available to hear them.

Science tells us that due to the nature of the cones in our eyes, we humans see less than one percent of the electromagnetic spectrum. This means that 99% of any environment we encounter remains unseen, filled with kaona.

Ancient Wisdom shows us that we do not only see with our eyes; every cell in our body is available for all manner of perception. In advanced training on this pathway, students in ancient times would be taught, for instance, to see with their skin, taste through sound, and smell with their eyes. Perceiving with the whole body awakens profound kaona of our existence.

In ancient times, the ability to decipher hidden meaning had less to do with knowledge and more to do with a depth of perception cultivated in the practitioner. It required a refined inner attention to perceive symbolic and mystical depths of a story or a teaching.

As I opened to the sensibilities of my perceptive field, allowing myself to receive information through my whole body, I found myself experiencing a much wider scope of perception. I was seeing with new eyes, and discovering that everything has endless depths waiting to be revealed. Everything was my teacher.

Situations, circumstances, relationships, emotions, perceptions, and experiences began to reveal 'hidden meanings' – new perspectives, understandings, possibilities, and revelations. These emerged in surprising ways from beneath my seemingly static, long-held patterns and assumptions. I came to realize that many kaona of each moment were alive if I was able to see them.

During my third training, the group was on a hilltop overlooking the magnificent undulating landscape of northern California. We were learning a practice to develop 360-degree vision, which began with extending our peripheral vision. Part way through the exercise, both my body and ability to pay attention were exhausted. Moments later, a hawk flew across my field of vision. I noticed it had a clear, pale but vibrant bright bubble around it forming a perfect circle a few feet beyond its wingspan. I was absorbed in the bird, and the unfamiliar glow that surround it, until it left my view. As the exercise continued, three more hawks passed before me, each one appearing in this clear, vibrant bubble, moving with them as they moved. By this time I had either lost track of any fatigue or it was gone. I was excited to be seeing something I had never seen before. By the end of the exercise, the trees on the horizon we were facing also seemed coated with a layer of brightness that was unfamiliar to me. My new perceptions arose from being engaged with my whole body through motion and attention. I was inhabiting my perceptive field which spontaneously revealed another kaona of Life, perhaps there all along, but which I had never witnessed.

Even though we are used to the narrow bandwidth of our learned perceptions, receiving the world through our entire perceptive field is our natural state of being. Whether we realize it or not, we are already perceiving through our whole system – all hundred trillion cells, every organ and organelle, every feeling, taste, and image – one hundred percent of the time. Our task is to open consciously to this natural state and expand the limitations of what we think we already know.

Where we place our attention is our choice. In any moment, we can choose to inhabit more of who we are by allowing ourselves to pay attention to the simplest aspects we can feel in the body: sensation, rhythm, image, movement, breath, shape, etc. We may discover that what we used to dismiss as insignificant is a profound opening to the infinite field of Life Itself.

"This work unblocks pathways in the brain through the body, reestablishing latent connections between past, present, and future, or body, mind and spirit. Developing greater sensitivity through experience of the physical body in specific motion. Here we enable ourselves to let go of our modern consciousness, the Western stoic reasoning, the freedom to give ourselves permission to truly feel our greatness as a human being – with an encompassment of compassionate humbleness and dignity."

— Kahu Abraham Kawai'i

◐ INTEGRATION EXERCISE • PERCEPTIVE FIELD

This Integration Exercise on page 108 offers an opportunity to approach your perceptive field in a deeply visceral way.

CHAPTER 6
CENTER OF THE UNIVERSE

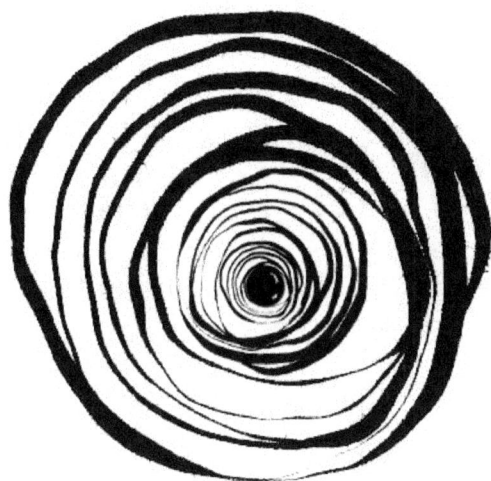

WHERE ARE WE?

We stand waiting
In this motion we call life
Not quite knowing where we are
Are we standing still
Or hurtling at a million miles per hour
Through space?

Are we filled with purpose
Or simply filling time?
Are we meeting Life
Or blotting it all out?

We stand waiting
For the Earth to move
For the winds to shift
For the sky to fall
For the end is near
And the time has come
For us to fall from our ignorant throne
To where we live
On the Earth
With the dirt
And the creatures
With the food and the waste
In the wetness and the desert.

Have we forgotten?

We stand waiting
For the earth to shake our minds loose
For the rain to pour through us
And wash away every hate-filled thought.

We stand waiting
For the fire to eat
What does not nourish
And leave us here
Or not here
Bitter
Or cleansed.

We wait
For someone to tell us
It's OK to breathe
To stand or run
To be afraid or safe.

Have we forgotten?

That we are Life Itself unfolding
That we are already home
In this moment
As it is
With the falling sky
And the shaking land.

Have we forgotten?

That Life will never fail us
That we are The Infinite
Trapped or Free
Lost or Listening
Here,
Or nowhere at all

—J. Mountain (2018)

A few years after my second training with Kahu, I faced an unexpected crisis in my life. My relationship with a longtime boyfriend had suddenly ended, I had no permanent place to live, and out of the blue, something extreme started to happen in my body. I was having numerous unusual sensations, including what felt like fireworks and explosions inside my blood vessels. My vision was altered. I was seeing layers of shape and movement in thin air. My energy was supercharged. I was on a constant 'high' and getting no sleep. I have never been attracted to consuming mind-altering substances, so my experiences were not induced by any chemical stimulant or substance, including alcohol, plant medicines, or marijuana.

I took a trip off-island to do sessions at a friend's place on the mainland, and the phenomenon in my body continued to accelerate. I wasn't sure how long I could live without sleep. After about two weeks, I started to become afraid that my nervous system would burn out. Not sure where to turn, I emailed Kahu and explained my situation.

To my surprise, he emailed me back with a very formal greeting explaining who he was, including his background and titles of accomplishment. He went on to state who he knew me to be, recounting some history of my presence in his workshops, and why he was even responding to my email. What followed became a long-distance, private training that lasted over a month. Kahu would give me specific physical and energetic practices to do each day, after which I was to email him and describe what was happening in my system.

The training was an unforgettable experience of welcoming and moving with the vast array of what was arising in me. Even though most of the exercises he gave me were completely unfamiliar, I felt safe under Kahu's guidance. His encouragement was to embrace it all rather than try to 'let it go'. In his words:

"Attempting to dislodge your situation at this time may not be advisable. Once gone, it may never return, and no matter how you might see it conceptually or consciously, in all the rules of life you place upon it, may well be that which prevents you from ever returning to the gates of creation. Call it what you may, Samadhi, Nirvana, Touch of the "Holy Spirit", if you dislodge it, then all you have in this life is the linear height of worldly concepts and inconclusive consciousness...... It is time to take your place alongside yourself, in the dignity of creation with aligned freedom of consciousness... It is time to "use" now, this which has come upon you, challenge death as you have challenged life in its reality."

I wasn't sure if he was using the word *death* symbolically or not. Was I dying to the old perceptions of who I knew myself to be, or did he mean I was challenging a physical death? I couldn't know. Whatever it was felt huge and beyond my ability to comprehend. I had no choice but to go directly through it, and dove wholeheartedly into the practices.

The exercises were rigorous and demanding. All I could do was take one day at a time, sometimes one moment at a time, to complete them, and email my report to Kahu while still working daily with clients.

I was navigating the unknown in a profoundly visceral way. With the tumultuous uprisings in my body, it did at times feel like I was, as Kahu said, challenging death. I trusted him implicitly and felt fortunate to have his guidance.

"It's nothing cosmic," he reassured me, "just the heights of physiology approaching the gates of spirituality... sensory, sensual, angelic love and feeling, earthly love and feeling, Divine creative sensitivities, all being unclassified, but felt and experienced in the Greatness and Dignity of Divine Compassion."

In total, the experience lasted thirty-seven days. By the end, the feeling of wild energy surges and explosions in my body was no longer there. It felt more like the process allowed these energies to erupt safely and to integrate in my system, rather than attempting to calm them down. It was clear that my previous sense of self had exploded along with it. My body felt strong and empty. My mind, just empty.

This period was, even to this day, the most intense experience of my life, offering multiple depths of teachings that took years to integrate.

During this training, one of the ancient principles that became deeply absorbed in my system was the discovery of a new grounding point. There was so much

going on inside of me, I was forced to find balance in the only place I could –
the Center of it all. I realized that every sensation, experience, reverberation,
landscape, emotion and event occurring inside and outside of me was landing in
my perception.

Even with Kahu's assistance, I was truly the only one who could decide to move
forward in the training. When the physical, emotional, and psychological stress
accelerated, I was the only one who could decide to continue.

I realized that it could not be any other way. We are the only ones receiving every
aspect of our lives, and, consciously or unconsciously, choosing how to navigate.
Regardless of the circumstances, ultimately the choices we make with our own
energy are the determining factors in our lives. Through our-moment-by moment
navigation, we are the creators of our own destiny.

This pivotal training gave me my first true awareness of living at the Center of my
Universe.

The principles of our universe that are in motion, from the rotation of the planets
to the subatomic levels of the body, point to what the Ancients identified as
"Natural Order".

A river flows from its source down the mountainside, filling the low places and
pooling, or eventually overflowing the high places and streaming into the ocean.
Plants, in the right conditions, grow from seeds, spores, or sprout from roots. The
universe, it is hypothesized, started with the big bang. We begin in the meeting of
ovum and sperm. Everything in Natural Order has an origin point.

The Ancients also recognized that every aspect of Life exists in its own universe.
and that everything is experiencing Life from its origin point at the center of
that universe. Looking out into the garden right now, I see that some leaves are
experiencing a warm, sunny day, while others, under the canopy of other trees, are
experiencing a cooler morning, still damp with dew. For some leaves, today will not

be a bright day. That is the reality of their unique perspective.

Cells, atoms, organs, molecules, plants, microbes, and every form of life, are each operating from their unique perspective at the center of their own existence even while moving in harmony with the whole. We are indeed made of, and surrounded by, universes within universes.

Modern humans in the Western world have mostly lost touch with Natural Order. We have been taught to look to an origin point outside of ourselves, and as a result, end up living life according to some external criteria, or at least our interpretation of it. In other words, we have somehow learned how to navigate life from a perspective that is outside of ourselves.

We dedicate our lives to the superficial, such as fashion, popularity, trendiness and status, or deeper aspects like doctrine, spiritual practices, gurus, intimate relationships, and everything in between.

Whether noble or profane, if the path we choose places our center outside of ourselves, we have lost our connection with Natural Order, and ultimately with our Source. We have fooled ourselves into thinking that these external origin points will give us what we are seeking, when what we are seeking has been inside of us all along. In some cases, we can make the grave mistake of sourcing ourselves in our personality: our belief systems, desires, preferences, and prejudices. In this case, we mistake our conditioned self for our true center.

The Natural Order of Ancient Wisdom remains true today: We are the only ones who can fully inhabit our own lives. We are the only ones experiencing each moment. We each live at the center of our unique perception.

As we cultivate our Perceptive Field, we become more aware of the many kaona arising inside and outside of us. Using ancient navigation, we can recognize everything that arises as a member of our internal Family.

As poet Anaïs Nin once said: "We don't see the world as it is. We see it as we are." Resting at the center of my universe, I can recognize myself in everything.

Placing our attention in our Perceptive Field requires a willingness to open to a spectrum of listening that cannot be quantified or defined by the brain. We must learn to be in receptivity to more than the narrow bandwidth we are used to hearing. We can think of this as a wider range of resonance. For example, listening only to our conscious mind is like listening only to the violin, or the tuba in a rich orchestral piece of music. Opening up to the resonance of the consciousness alive through our Perceptive Field allows us to hear the whole symphony in its vibrant, textural fullness. We experience the audible landscape of the whole ecosystem of the forest, rather than just the sound of one bird.

According to the Ancients, all that is arriving in us is alive with mana or life force energy. As we open our awareness to receive the layers of Life in our system at any given moment, we allow that energy to open and to flow through us. We begin to participate in this meeting with Life from the Center of our Universe. This is the only place from which we can move forward. We can pretend, but we can never *actually* move forward in our lives from a center that is not our own.

Through the body, the Ancients guide us in adjusting our vantage point. Where are we perceiving *from*? Are we in the narrow point of view of one of our inner children? Are we centered in the expectations, opinions, or beliefs of the outside world? Where we are seeing from determines the quality of our vision. Cultivating an awareness of where we are sourcing ourselves in any given moment can be a powerful and transformative practice.

As we nourish this practice of resting in The Center of our Universe, it becomes a portal for more and more Life to emerge. We are able to meet and claim more of who we areand cultivate harmony in our internal world. Our experience of what comes to meet us in life changes in response to our new resonance.

Instead of our limited perceptions struggling to make sense of the world outside, every encounter becomes an opportunity to deepen our awareness, and to move forward on the path. We begin to embody an endless convergence of Life meeting Life. All of the energy we wasted on blaming the outside world can be reclaimed to expand our compassion for ourselves and others.

"Should the pattern of your thoughts come into a similar rhythm with your heart, and your heart rhythm with your breath, your emotions with your sense of feel, taste, smell and hearing, you then experience a breakaway of old concepts and old patterns. All things, functions, and thoughts will certainly move into a new space of accelerated conscious continuum. When you find yourself in the Center of your Universe, then you have arrived. Where the universe can now find you."

— Kahu Abraham Kawai'i

This guided meditative journey on page 110 brings us into an experience of resting at the Center of our Universe.

CHAPTER 7
HO'OPONOPONO

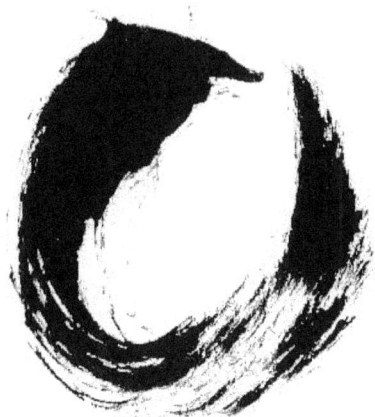

HEAVEN

Heaven is here
When I can see with a Clear Heart.
When I remember
my Breath.

Heaven is here
When Fear is my Friend
Instead of my Enemy.
When I recognize all enemies
As my own longing
For Wholeness.

Heaven is here
When I forget to remember
That I'm supposed to be
Someone.

Heaven is here
When I remember
That I am Life,
And that All Life
Is my Family.

Heaven is here
When my Family
Stands Together
As One Heart
One Song
One Motion.

Heaven is
Holding each other close
Half an Earth
Away,
Because
We cannot be apart.

As I open my eyes,
Heaven remembers Itself.

— J. Mountain (2015)

The Hawaiian word Ho'oponopono means to "make right" or to bring into balance that which has been out of balance. Ho'oponopono is an ancient healing practice designed to restore harmony in relationships within the family, company, village, and even between nations. There are many deeply traditional and long-practiced forms of Ho'oponopono that are passed directly from the elders.

Traditionally, the respected expert, or Kahuna Ho'oponopono, works closely and extensively with the wronged parties involved in conflict, skillfully moderating in a series of highly stylized formal steps to resolution, always with much prayer and regular clarification. The process often takes many hours. Depending on the severity of the situation, this kind of Ho'oponopono can sometimes take days, weeks, months, or years to come to resolution. The results include essentially a summary statement, mutual understanding, and some form of a settlement where applicable, with peace and harmony prevailing – the ultimate goal.

In addition, Hawaiian families traditionally had their own daily Ho'oponopono performed together with all family members in attendance, often prior to sharing the family meal. This ensured a clearing of the air of grievances and problems, then celebrating life together in harmony with each other. In this form, the matriarch or patriarch served as the moderator. Training in this daily practice was far less extensive than the village Kahuna Ho'oponopono, but no less significant.

Another form of Ho'oponopono was conducted in ancient times when someone in the village was sick. For the ceremony, everyone in the village would gather in a circle with the sick person lying down in the middle. Each person would be called upon to speak out any grievances they were holding – anger, resentment, fear, mistrust, betrayal – toward their children, spouse, leaders of the village, priests, or Gods. Once everyone had spoken, the Kahuna priest, or leader of the ceremony, would offer up all the grievances in a prayer of recognition and clearing. After this process, the person in the middle would be healed.

The Ancients knew that no one in the village was operating in a vacuum. Each person was an intricate part of the whole. Any conflict within one part of the organism of the village meant that the whole organism had to come together to find healing.

Today, there are modern adaptations of Ho'oponopono that lead us through a process of forgiveness. The most popular one I know of came through the work of Kahuna Morna Simeone and offers the phrases: "Thank you. I'm sorry. Please forgive me. I love you". This can be a powerful process that allows us to embrace discord and free it.

In the paradigm of Ke Ala Hōkū, we are guided first toward making peace with the 'Ohana within before attempting to heal any relationships with others.

In the past, I have practiced forgiveness in many different ways. Sometimes, even after I felt that the issue was resolved internally, my experience would tell me otherwise. I remember once going through a particularly painful breakup with a partner. After practicing the popular form of Ho'oponopono, energy medicine and journaling, I thought I was complete and had forgiven him and the whole situation. A few months later, however, I ran into him and was surprised to feel hurt and angry all over again. I had forgiven him in my mind, but my memories and emotions had not been resolved. Apparently, my forgiveness had been theoretical and not embodied.

Realizing that I had spent my time focusing solely on the outer relationship, I began all over again, this time meeting the internal 'Ohana of my hurt and anger, bringing them closer instead of trying to make them go away. With no immediate goal of resolution in mind, my task was to welcome these difficult internal Family Members, in the form of my own feelings, and allow them to fully express themselves. I was surprised by what arose. The hurt let me know that it was born long before this relationship. Images arose from my childhood, where years of perceived rejection by my peers had created deep wounds. The anger revealed my own desperation to be loved, and my deep feeling that this would never be possible.

I was finally able to see these internal Family Members in their fullness and own them as my creations, ignited by the specific circumstances of the relationship. My ex-boyfriend was no longer the source of my pain. I had found peace in allowing what was true to rise in me, to feel it fully, and to own it. Between he and I, ultimately, there was nothing to forgive.

The ancients knew that everything was vibration. Quantum physics recognizes that, indeed, everything is in motion at the atomic level. This includes every aspect of our human existence. Even the quality of our relationships with each member of our internal family creates a resonance. As we vibrate this into the world, it is reciprocated in kind. The harmony or disharmony that we experience, consciously or unconsciously, finds its match in our living experience. In this paradigm, what we experience coming from the outside world is neither good nor bad, but a resonant match to our own relationship with ourselves.

On this Pathway, practicing Ho'oponopono asks us to find that matching dynamic inside of our own Internal Family. If there is outer conflict, we can ask: "How am I fighting myself? What voices inside me put me down or diminish my accomplishments? What parts of my Internal 'Ohana don't really love the other parts?"

Note that this is not an exploration of how I am in relation to the world around me. That is certainly a valid practice, but this version of Ho'oponopono brings us to the vibrational root of the conflict. It uncovers the relationships in our internal 'Ohana that manifest their energetic equivalent in our external reality.

By feeling into the wider vibration instead of the specifics, we can reveal the vibration inside of us that is a match and meet it with compassion. For example, if a partner betrays you and is not honest about it, you could look inside and ask, "What parts of me betray other parts of myself?" It could be that your need to please your parents by staying in an unhappy job betrays your real desire to be an artist. You could discover that you haven't been honest with yourself about how unhappy your creative self has been with your rigid work ethic. The details are completely different from the external circumstance, but they are a resonant match.

This work offers us the chance to take responsibility for everything that arises in us, as well as everything that comes toward us. As we recognize more hurt and disconnected parts of ourselves, we practice the internal navigation of bringing them closer and allowing them to speak in the embrace of our Head of Household, the wise, expansive being at our core. By allowing each Family Member a voice, and a place in our 'Ohana, we set that energy free. Finally heard, it no longer has to rattle the bars of its cage or knock louder on the door of our awareness through an external situation. We enter a constant practice of bringing more harmony to our internal world, which overflows into the world around us.

In this way, every moment, situation, and circumstance is an offering to discover and to embrace more aspects of who we are. In our adult life, what arises in the external world arises as a gift of awareness.

On this Pathway, then, the journey toward Ho'oponopono – making things right – begins inside of us. It asks us to come back to the pure expression of Life that we are. All of Nature exists in a great embrace of every aspect of itself. If we allow that same Nature within us to be free, it will guide us to the same place – to an embrace of every aspect of who we are, as well as everything that comes to meet us.

As we participate in this kaona of Ho'oponopono, at the origin points of any dissonance inside ourselves, we transmute our own deepest hurt, including the anger and self-destructive behavior that can accompany it, into harmony. The battles waging within us can finally come to peace.

Approaching the world from this place means that we both emit and attract more harmony in our lives. Others begin to respond differently to us, and the story of our habitual patterns begins to change. We start to live in a different world because we have changed the resonant call from deep inside.

As we free our internal discord, it is not what we do in the world, but who we are, on a vibrational level, that becomes the seed of peace. From the personal to the global, we humans are the poison, the creators of discord, and we are the medicine.

Aloha: *The acceptance of everything inside of us and compassion for all that exists.*

⟲ INTEGRATION EXERCISE · HO'OPONOPONO

This Integration Exercise on page 111 offers a Ceremony of one form of Ho'oponopono that you may do to restore harmony in your relationships with others or with your own Internal Family..

CHAPTER 8
ANCIENT LOMI LOMI

A CLIENT'S EXPERIENCE OF ANCIENT LOMI LOMI

The session seemed to take me through many portals, some personal pain and residues and then mainly through layers of generations. As you worked on my back and energy released I saw the centuries of what people have done to others in the name of God, religion, and against women... I saw many scenes like clips from different times; the main theme was how I felt the agony of injustice and how people destroy others... Indigenous people and women were the strongest images. I know this heritage in my ancestry and feel I connected more deeply to the deep sorrow of bearing witness to and being part of such a narrative of collective abuse.

There was a point when I felt all the ancient ancestors who were like keepers of an ancient wisdom came or maybe I arrived in their presence and they greeted me as if they had been expecting me. It was like a homecoming; I felt welcomed and at peace as if at the end of a long journey. Then I became the open flower – my whole body felt like a wild orchid.... then as if I was the river and then the ocean... at one. I felt I was nature in a way that I have not felt so deeply before. This still moves me so much to think about now. It felt like a communion and unity from the deepest place within... where I dissolved and was at one with nature.

— C.H. • Ancient Lomi Lomi Recipient

There are many streams and lineages of Lomi Lomi. What I call "Ancient Lomi Lomi" is the modern form of Lomi Ke Ala Hōkū. As practiced today, it does not take place in a *heiau* (temple) and does not last from ten hours up to fifteen days. Its essence, however, is the resonance found on the Pathway to the Stars.

The work itself is alive. Our job then, as practitioners, is to keep coming back to each living moment. As we drop more deeply into our bodies, we begin to come into a deeper relationship with our Cellular Being. Our listening and ability to respond becomes more refined. We are guided by our Perceptive Field rather than the limited knowing of our conditioned mind. This means that we are following Life rather than leading it. We are receiving and responding to shape, breath, texture, flow and natural rhythm. These are the gateways to cellular presence that bring us to the threshold of the infinite within us.

Internally, we are in a state of allowing. Whatever arises – image, memory, thought, or emotion – is welcome. As we embrace and move with them, the depth and quality of our presence becomes more complete. We recognize more Life in us and move with it. The quality of our touch changes in response to this Life, and the session vibrates with the fullness of the present moment in the many kaona arising. We welcome whatever arises because it is alive.

The practitioner rests in the midst of shapes, sensations, emotions, images, colors, rhythms, textures, temperatures, motion and breath, all the whisperings of the Mystery pouring through us. Whether our minds perceive the moment to be magical, mundane, or even challenging, we accept each inner Family Member and remain grounded in the flow of Life through the motion and alignment of the bodywork.

These shifts in perception change our essential resonance and, as Kahu called it, "raise our internal speed". We begin to vibrate with Life and enter the flow, rhythm, and resonance of Creation. It is at the threshold of this resonance that the bodywork of Ancient Lomi Lomi is performed.

The session begins with *Kahi*, meaning "One", a practice of laying on of hands in which we bring our attention to the origin point inside our own bodies: the stars.

Like many forms of Lomi Lomi the bodywork is made up of long, flowing strokes with the forearms. and may contain deep work with the elbow or hands. Among other techniques, it can include organ massage, joint rotations, and facial work. The motion around the table is guided by *Ka'alele 'au* (Flying), in which the practitioner is embodying the shape and motion of the Infinite through a specific dance-like motion.

Guided by principles of attention which cultivate specific alignment, motion, breath, and present moment awareness, practitioners finds themselves continually coming back to the motion of Life inside themselves, and to the meeting place with another vast universe, embodied by the person on the table.

Lomi Ke Ala Hōkū, and consequently 'Ancient Lomi Lomi', has no intention. The ancient practitioners were not concerned with any agenda to fix, calm, enlighten, or change the recipient in any way. They moved in the resonance of their internal speed. This resonance itself calls out to the pure Life in the recipient, and as both meet, beyond conceptual awareness, the dynamic alchemy of Life meeting Life emerges.

The music for each client is created based on their ancestral lineage and is combined with Hawaiian and world music. It is a significant part of the session, played loud enough to vibrate the cells of the body. Both practitioner and recipient swim in the potent resonance of the music – the sound of our beginnings, our ancestors, our gifts, our potential.

Recipients find themselves with space to feel more of who they are. As the resonant call of the work awakens in their Cellular Being, each person's system will generate a unique experience. Sometimes this means that old, unresolved aspects, memories, and emotions arise. Others have mystical experiences of being in another time and space, or receive visions, guidance or clarity. Some fall asleep, or float in and out of altered states, allowing for a deep receptivity throughout their system. Often recipients experience a combination of responses, as an undulating journey unfolding from deep inside.

The consciousness of the entire body is the recipient of this flowing touch through which much sensory information can be ignited. However, it is important to note that sessions of Ancient Lomi Lomi are not sexual. Private areas remain draped for the entire session. Recipients may feel this vital energy rising and are encouraged to allow it to move through them, just as they would any other sensation, emotion, or thought. Allowing the whole system to speak and be heard as living energy, without attempting to manipulate any aspect is a crucial component of the work.

When we touch another human being, we are not only touching what we know of as anatomy – skin, muscle, tendon, bone, fascia, etc. – we are touching a whole universe of both conscious and unconscious impressions, memories, emotions, patterns, belief systems, and experiences spanning the spectrum of human existence. As practitioners, we cannot know what each particular person needs for their optimum evolution. Their system, however, knows, and given the chance, it will reveal its unique offering in the language of Life Itself. When we operate from our desire to help or from our analytical knowledge base, we interfere with this deep and intrinsic natural process.

Our task as practitioners is not to move toward the recipient, even with our lofty ideas of love and healing, but to back up into alignment with the Life inside of ourselves, which will allow for a connectedness with all of Life. If we can stay in this alignment, we will find ourselves meeting the ancient soul of our own body – the pure Life that animates us all.

That Life is alive and conscious. It is listening. It is responding. When we can place ourselves in an attention that recognizes this living Being inside, we find ourselves at the edge of infinity, the edge of the unknown, stepping across the line into a new perception of ourselves and the world over and over again. We arrive in a state of discovery rather than intellectual knowing.

Every moment of our lives is an opportunity to cultivate this pathway, to move in cooperation with Life. Every session receives us already open in this field of receptivity and willingness to feel all of who we are.

When I was first training in the work, I received many sessions that seemed to open up new landscapes, horizons and possibilities inside of me. I saw and felt things I had never seen or felt before. In one memorable session, I clearly saw face after face, seemingly hundreds of men, women, and children of many different ages and ethnicities, all moving their mouths as if speaking to me, but without sound. Their images appeared against a black background, flashing in faster and faster succession in my mind's eye. Although I'm not a person who frequently sees many images inside, their faces were crystal clear. Even though I couldn't identify what it was about, I had the feeling they were all telling a story that they had been waiting to tell for a very long time.

Accompanying the visions was a turbulence in my system, like something in me had been ignited, or a dam had been broken, and the water was rushing through me, finding its free flow. The motion and myriad of emotions were indescribable, but included feelings of excitement and recognition of some long-lost connection. Even though I couldn't identify it, something deep in me had been met and was responding.

I learned later of the possibility that these could have been the faces and energies of my ancestors. The session may have offered them an opening to come forward and be recognized in me. Even if these weren't truly my ancestors appearing, I believe they were aspects of my Being that wanted to speak in vivid and powerful ways. It is a session I will never forget.

———————————————

The bodywork of Ancient Lomi Lomi, or Lomi Ke Ala Hōkū, is essentially a by-product of the Pathway to the Stars. It is one avenue through which to cultivate our embodied Presence. It springs from the profound work of refining our internal speed in every moment of our lives. This ever-deepening Pathway, of meeting ourselves and navigating from a space of acceptance, expands our perception and leads us toward a life of infinite discovery.

This way of being can transform the way we move in the world, and how we experience the world coming toward us. Endless discovery, transmutation, and freedom become a way of life. Sometimes we may find ourselves in a period of discovery that can last for weeks, months or years. Transmutation may feel like walking through a fire or lingering in a void and can also last for varying periods of time. Wherever we are, we can choose to meet the kaona of each present moment in fullness.

We may realize that even in this simple moment, in this single breath, this choice to meet whatever arises as a part of who we are, we open a doorway of healing for ourselves and for all of humanity. Through our conscious embodiment, we hold the potential to free the past, and transform the future.

As Mahatma Gandhi said, we step into the possibility to "Be the change we wish to see in the world".

Whatever is to be born is born in you. Whatever is to be remembered is remembered in you. Like your foot meeting the undulating shape of the ground in every step, part of you is in constant unity with what is, beyond conceptual thought. Our powerful attention can rest in this place. Every cell in us contains the whispers of Ancient Wisdom. We are not limited by the definitions of our conditioned minds. We are Life in motion, waiting to be heard. This wider spectrum of Life is the teacher. We can only be the student – listening."
— Jody Mountain

This exercise offers a new experience of bodywork. Follow the attention offered in this integration work on page 114 to open to expanded sensibility of your cellular being.

CHAPTER 9
RESONANCE OF A NEW PARADIGM

IN A TREE HOUSE *(excerpt)*

Light
Will someday split you open
Even if your life is now a cage...
Love will surely bust you wide open
Into an unfettered blooming new galaxy...
......A life-giving radiance will come...
From a sacred crevice
in your body
A bow rises each night
And shoots your soul into God...
— Hafiz

Mystics throughout the ages have guided us toward our innate connection with Spirit. Evolving as we have through our segmented mental structures, we have seemingly captured this idea of ourselves as Spiritual Beings and separated it from our existence as physical beings.

Ancient Wisdom points us toward the unity of all Being. It offers us a worldview in which we can begin to see that the Earth is one unified consciousness. On a different kaona, we as individuals are also one unified being. The entire spectrum of our thoughts, emotions, memories, perceptions, sensations, breath, heartbeat, chemistry, physiology, electromagnetic field, energetic field, movement, stillness, belief systems, and spirit are all here, now, vibrating seamlessly through every cell. And all are intimately connected with every seemingly insignificant motion we make: the way we hold ourselves, move, speak, breathe, sleep, even what we see and remember.

When we find our way back to our unity, we will begin to restore The Ancient Soul of the Body, and our interconnectedness with all of Life.

In the eyes of the work, the "unfettered blooming new galaxy" that Hafiz speaks about is within. To the Ancients, it is the limitless Life that animates us. That Life is constantly in the motion of union, of dynamic balance and blossoming harmony throughout our system. We are not just minds seeking for God. We are all of it: body, mind, emotions, spirit, hopes, dreams, memories, sensations, vibrations, awarenesses, fears, regrets, longing – all of it, in one seamless Whole. The voice of this One, from deep below our conscious mind, is the bow that "rises each night, and shoots your soul into God."

The Ancients tell us that we do not have to live separated from this innate Life that is, alive every moment of every day, in motion with us and for us.

We are not here in this life as a thought, a moral code or belief system. These are only ideas. We are here as a living embodiment of Spirit, inhabiting all that we are in each moment. When we start to welcome the diversity within, leaving no part of ourselves behind, we begin to reawaken our original state of Being in all of the dimensions that we exist.

Ke Ala Hōkū, the Pathway to The Stars, is, at its essence, quite simple. It is founded in the practice of listening to the essential life force of the body as an equal or even more evolved consciousness than what our brain is able to perceive.

It is our minds that are complicated. To arrive in a state of inclusion, respect, and honor for all that we are, we come up against our familial, social and religious programming. We also come face-to-face with the programming of humanity. Having been taught for millennia that God or Source is located somewhere outside of ourselves, the possibility that the Divine can be found in the body seems almost blasphemous.

We have forgotten, however, that the Divine inhabits all that is. Awakening the Ancient Soul of the Body is the recognition that living, breathing consciousness itself flows through every atom, cell, tissue, organ, organelle, and all that arises in this sacred container. As we allow this Infinite Force more space in our awareness, we discover a world of vibrancy, possibility, and well-being. In the simple listening to our embodied being, we enter the realm of the miraculous.

At the waters edge one pristine morning, I was overwhelmed by the experience, moved by the vibrant colors, the texture in my feet meeting sand, my skin being touched by the breeze – the simplicity of Life moving in such beautiful ways and landing in my awareness, my perception. A thought passed through me – something that I had heard somewhere before – "Life is here for us".

Indeed, it seems true that the Earth, plants, air, sun, ocean and all their natural ecosystems support Life. They nurture our well-being and our very existence. I sat for a moment in gratitude that no matter what the trappings of our outer life look like, we are fully supported. Life Itself is always here for all of us.

If we observe nature, we can witness it's incredible generosity. Everything just gives. The natural regenerative energy at the center of the Earth continues to make its way to the surface and create new land. A healthy soil continues to nurture healthy plants, and the sun shines ceaselessly allowing our oceans to remain liquid, helping to sustain our atmosphere, and feeding every living thing on Earth.

There is nothing in nature that is not an offering to the rest of Life. Even a forest fire offers new regenerative material to the soil, and an earthquake resets the alignment of the Earth's crust. In the midst of that continuous giving is also receiving, resulting in a deeply harmonious interconnectedness. Life is meeting Itself in complete and utter generosity, through many different forms.

As I sat, and my senses continued to expand, a feeling arose that "I am also here for Life". This took me by surprise. Why had I never seen this before? The natural motion of the Life inside of me is also an expression of this generosity of being.

Through the perception of Western Mind, my belief systems center around concepts like: being a good person, including: "It's better to give than to receive", and ideas that have been elevated in our society like selflessness. While there is nothing at all wrong with these ideas, they can easily come from doctrine, belief systems and perhaps enlightened teachers that we are drawn to emulate. We become focused on the resulting behavior instead of the living journey of Spirit.

The pure Life inside of us guides us to a natural generosity that includes our own being.

This energy, just like the external nature around us, is not calculating in its generosity. It is fulfilling its natural expression as Life Itself. Meeting the Life inside of us, and allowing it more space, motion, and voice, will guide us toward a generosity of Spirit we may not have thought possible. We become instruments of Life, not by trying to emulate a noble idea, but by embodying the Spirit that we are.

As Life Itself, I am an offering. You are an offering. The work guides us to source ourselves in a place inside that does not decide what that offering will be, but simply allows it.

This Pathway is both ancient and revolutionary. As we begin to shift our origin point back to the inherent Life in all things, we reverberate in the realm of the Sacred in all that we do. Coming back into relationship with the forgotten parts of ourselves, both inside of us and in our environment, we create a revolution of health and vitality for all aspects of our world – the Earth, our fellow creatures, and all of humanity.

———————————————

Our old ways of seeing and being may feel lost as we free fall into a new world. We must be willing let go of our moorings, what keeps us tethered to the familiar, and set sail on uncharted seas. What beckons us is a remembering of what we arrived on this Earth knowing. It is a beckoning to freedom, the resonance of a new paradigm awakening.

In keeping with Ancient Wisdom, this new paradigm is also alive! As we move toward it, it will move toward us, and together, we will evolve as Life remembering Itself.

———————————————

"Think about it, and it will think about you.
Live it and it will live for you.
Apply it in any direction,
and it will apply itself in that direction for you.
Praise it and it will praise you.
There is nothing that it will not do for you,
inasmuch as you would do for yourself.
Always hold the greatest thoughts about anyone, anything or anyplace,
especially toward yourself.
For the natural rule is, if any,
that YOU will always be the recipient."
— Kahu Abraham Kawai'i

Take this opportunity to imagine a strikingly new and beautiful world, waiting just below the surface of your awareness. This integration exercise can be found on page 115.

Integration Exercises

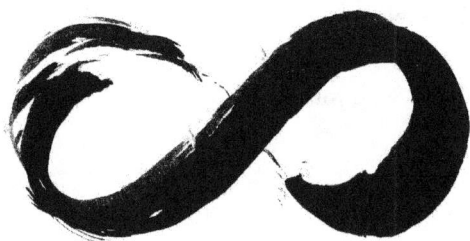

Set a timer for 15 minutes and sit quietly in a comfortable position. Pay attention to an easy, effortless breath.

Let your mind gently know that you are not looking for anything, and invite it to take a rest. You can even visualize placing a blanket over your brain and tucking it in for a nap.

Continue to breathe easily and allow yourself to become receptive to any sensations that arise. It could be the heaviness of your seat or legs on the ground, the rhythm of your breath, the saliva in your mouth.

If your mind wants to analyze or comment, gently lead it back to it's nap and cover your brain again with the blanket.

Stay with your breath and with your sensations.

Unless you're in pain or discomfort, don't try to fix or change anything, and keep coming back to a state of allowing.

Drop into a deep listening. The language of the body will not be in words. You may experience sensations, emotions, images, rhythms, colors, textures as part of your journey. Don't try to interpret them. Just allow them to keep rising.

If you feel numb just stay with your listening, and allow that to rise with your easy breath.

It's quite possible that your mind might become bored. This is natural as there is nothing here for the mind, which usually loves stimulation. Keep coming back to the breath and the subtle feelings in the body without interpretation.

Practicing this meditation first thing in the morning or just before bed will allow you to begin to awaken and strengthen the ability to listen to the miracle of the body's consciousness. This is an infinite door leading to the direct experience of your own Spirit, awake in the body.

INTEGRATION EXERCISE • THE BODY IS ALIVE

After years, or even decades of familiarity, it can be challenging to see our body in a new way. Use the Integration Exercise below to imagine new possibilities. Find the play in pretending that this is possible, even if you don't necessarily believe it. You will be speaking in the language of the body, which every body part, organ, organ system, hair follicle, structure, tissue, cell, organelle, hormone, shape, rhythm, proton, electron, atom, quark, bio-photon, neuron, texture, and sensation will hear.

Spend at least 10 minutes in this imaginative world.

INTEGRATION • IMAGINE

Find a comfortable relaxed position, preferably lying on your back.

Imagine for a moment you are being shown a different version of your body than the one you may already know. In your imagination, take a look at your body lying on the floor as if from above. Notice that you can 'see' inside your body, all the way down to the cellular level. See a tremendous amount of movement, rhythm and energy as blood moves through the vessels and cellular processes vibrate with activity.

You might view it like a bee hive or a vibrant landscape with a huge variety of movement and activity.

Spend some time seeing or imagining your internal environment full of color, landscapes and movement of energy. See and feel the whole community buzzing and moving, or follow one of the beings on its pathway. Let the images come rather than trying to make them up. Nothing has to make sense as you immerse yourself in this other world.

Imagine now that each Being in your vision is alive with consciousness, not a mechanical 'intelligence', but actual beingness. Just like you are a unique person on

a planet of 8 billion people, imagine each tiny cell is a Being in it's own right.
Let the vision unfold as it does, and afterwards notice if there are any new or subtle
sensations, or changes in breath or awareness.

INTEGRATION EXERCISE • 'OHANA NUI

After asking permission, find a tree that would be willing to participate in this exercise.

Sit or stand a few feet away from the tree, facing it, and close your eyes. Feel into your breath, body and sensations.

Allow any emotions, images, or memories to arise and pass through you. When you feel complete, stand or sit with as much of your back as possible touching the tree.

Open again to feeling sensation, breath and body.

Notice what may be arising now as you and the tree meet.

Imagine that this tree is a new brother, sister, mother, father, or grandparent that you didn't know existed. Does anything in you change?

Notice.

Can you feel yourself and the tree breathing as one?

Take a moment several times during the day to slow down and recognize which of your internal Family Members are speaking. Just a simple pause and recognition will do.

At the end of the day, write down which Family Members arose. There may have been a sigh of bewilderment, a clenching of the jaw from frustration or a gasp of surprise. It doesn't matter if you can't identify the why. You may notice shoulder tension, a churning stomach or thirst as well as familiar emotions like frustration, insecurity or sadness. Just record what you notice without any explanation or analysis necessary.

Before you go to bed, call upon the Family Members you noticed during the day. Address them as you would living people. Let them know you noticed them today and that you are present and listening for anything else they would like to share.

Go to sleep without thinking too much about them. Be open to noticing even subtle changes in your experience. You may have a dream, or wake up with a song in your head, or have an impulse to go for a long walk or eat a certain type of food.

You may not think the response has anything to do with your observations, but just continue to follow your body and stay open to the possibilities. Feel your way along the Path.

Did you notice a different type of attention when relating to your inner world (thoughts, emotions, perceptions) as Members of your internal Family? If so, how was your attention different? Whether you felt a difference or not, write down what you perceived in your inner world. Did you notice any Family Members arising more frequently, or with more enthusiasm? Write down which ones you noticed and how they expressed themselves.

Noticing more frequent family members can help you identify some of your habitual responses to life, or your "default settings."

Find some access to nature outside – even a window will do. If you can be outside, this may be helpful. Simply observe what you notice in the landscape, and then switch your attention to feel inside your body. What do you feel, see or experience? For example, if you are looking at the clouds, notice what your initial perception is. For many of us it would be the simple identification of the clouds, and an observation of their movements, shapes, or colors.

Then take the time to feel more deeply in your body. Notice any emotions, changes of rhythm in your breath or heartbeat, any sensations in your body, changes in your temperature, any feeling in the bottom of your feet, or any changes at all in your body as you gaze. Notice the shift in attention from the external world to how it is being received by your system. See if you can notice what you're feeling without trying to analyze or change anything.

For instance, if you're feeling sad when you look at the clouds, don't try to figure out why you're feeling sad all of a sudden. Just feel what you feel as you observe these clouds. You might feel a grumbling in your belly. You might feel an uneasiness in your solar plexus. You might feel a deep sense of peace. You might notice your heartbeat slowing down or speeding up. Whatever you notice, don't make it right or wrong. Don't look for anything in particular. Simply notice the sometimes subtle difference between our face-value perceptions and what might be occurring inside ourselves that we normally might not pay attention to – the hidden experience of the same moment in our inner world.

If you have the opportunity to stand outside on the ground, do that in your bare feet, if possible. First notice your initial perception or reaction. Some of us land initially on the intellectual knowing of where we are and what we're doing, and remain there: "I'm standing barefoot on the grass." Drop into your sensations. The temperature might be cold, the grass might feel mushy in your feet. Continue to listen to what else might be arising in your body, emotions, memories. Allow any emotions or sensations you didn't expect, to rise. Again, without analysis or an attempt to fix or change, simply feel what you feel, notice what you notice.

Try this exercise in a few different environments if they're available. In this simple way, we begin to touch the edges of the living concept of *kaona* – the depths of being in any internal or external environment through a shift of attention. This exercise will serve to expand the possibilities in participation with Life.

◉ INTEGRATION EXERCISE • CENTER OF YOUR UNIVERSE

This exercise is best experienced in nature, anywhere you can lie down. Lying in a grassy area, or on the beach would be ideal. If that's not practical, you can also do this sitting somewhere in nature, like a on park bench, or on the ground.

Find a comfortable place somewhere in nature and close your eyes.

Before you shift your attention, check to see how you are perceiving. It's likely that when you hear a sound, your mind identifies that sound and goes outward to the source. When you feel the sun, you know instantly what it is, and again the mind may go outward to the idea or the location of the sun.

Gradually bring your attention inside your body. Notice the movement of the breath, the rhythm of your heart, the weight of your body sitting or lying down. Notice any sensations in your skin, for example the feeling of it being touched by the wind or the sun.

See if you can keep your attention only on the body and not on outside stimuli. Regardless of what you know is happening on the outside, what do you feel in your body? Notice the urge to identify or conceptualize your experience, and keep coming back to your visceral experience, what you are actually experiencing : i.e. warmth, texture, weight, sensation.

Switch your perspective from noticing the birds singing, for instance, to noticing how the sound meets your sense of hearing. Notice anything that the sound evokes in your sensations or emotions.

In other words, notice all the ways you are receiving the world around you. Notice that you are now resting in the center of your experience. You are inhabiting your Perceptive Field (not just your mind) and allowing everything to arrive in your system. You are resting at the Center of your Universe.

☯ INTEGRATION EXERCISE • HO'OPONOPONO

Find a person who is willing to be the 'blank screen' on to which you imagine someone with whom you are seeking resolution. (You may also use a willing tree or plant if another person is unavailable). If you're working with a person, they should commit to maintaining a neutral expression, devoid of responses like comments, advice or sympathy. The most effective way to practice this is for them to remain neutral, giving you an opportunity to see someone else in their place.

Looking into their eyes, or imagining eyes before you, see the eyes of the person with whom you have discord and say out loud everything that has been unsaid. Let all the feelings of hurt, anger, betrayal, disappointment, confusion, etc. speak. Address the chosen individual in the first person rather than telling a story. Say everything you have been holding inside, everything you have been afraid to say. Tell the truth about how you have felt and maybe even the reasons why you felt it was impossible to say those things before.

This is an opportunity for any internal family member that has been afraid, traumatized, suppressed, or frozen to express themselves. Do your best to say what you feel, rather than what you think of them or of the situation.

Although it should feel as real as possible, like you are actually speaking to them, the communication is actually within your own perception. You will in no way be 'hurting' the person you are addressing. The primary function of this form of Ho'oponopono is to free internal family members that have never had a chance to speak and to to finally express what has been secret, hidden away or forbidden. The entire ritual is happening inside the parameters of your own perceptions.

Give yourself permission to express yourself freely.

When you are complete, both parties should close their eyes for a few breaths and place their open attention on what is here now: sensations, emotions, breath, etc. If this is a mutual exercise, when both people are ready to open their eyes, the second person can begin to speak, using the above guidelines.

When you are both complete and after you have closed your eyes for a few minutes, open your eyes and together, say the words below while maintaining eye contact.

This prayer of resolution is not fixed but should contain references to emotions and thoughts specific to your particular sharing. Here is one possible version:

"Dear Mother
Dear Father
Dear Brother
Dear Sister
Dear Friend
Dear Partner
Dear Daughter
Dear Son
Dear part of myself
Dear Life
Dear God,

I am so so sorry for any ways in which I hurt you
And I am so so sorry for any ways in which you hurt me.
I believe that all we really wanted was to love and to be loved.
But somehow, this became distorted, misunderstood, confused.
I am sorry I lost my way.
I am sorry you lost your way.
We were doing the best we could with what we had at the time.
Thank you for all the opportunities you have given me to see myself
To learn and to grow
Even though it may have been painful sometimes.
Right now, it is time to set you free
To set myself free.
I now give back to you everything I may have taken from you
I now give back to you your anger, violence, confusion, desperation, resentment, lies [etc.]
I now give back all that belongs to you.
And I now call back to myself anything I may have left in your field

112

I now call back my innocence, joy, trust, strength, self-esteem, security, resilience, hurt, shame, frustration [etc.]
I take back all that belongs to me.
Everything magnetically returns to its rightful origin.
Right now.

I cut all unhealthy cords between us, leaving only the cords of Love that bind everything in the universe.
(clap together 3 times)

I am free.
You are free.
I wish you well.
So good-bye.
We are free."

(clap together 3 times)

Sit quietly for as long as you like.
Thank your partner for their participation.

INTEGRATION EXERCISE • ANCIENT LOMI LOMI

If you are comfortable receiving bodywork, find a practitioner that you resonate with, or get a recommendation from a friend and book an appointment.

During the session, no matter what kind of bodywork it is, practice feeling your own body, rather than the touch of the other person.*

(*Be sure to let your Massage Therapist know that you'd rather not have any talking during the session, so you can go more deeply into yourself.)

Practice letting go into a diffuse attention. Instead of following the practitioners movements, allow yourself to receive what arises in your system: any sensations, emotions, colors or images. Let them rise and fall as they do, without chasing them, or grabbing them with your mind.

Practice feeling the weight of your body sink into the table and allow yourself to fall asleep if you find yourself letting go in that way.

Later, write down your memories and observations of the session, even those images or feelings you don't necessarily understand. For example, colors, shapes, images, sensations, emotions, memories, changes in breath or heartbeat rhythm, changes in the rhythm of your thoughts, etc.

Welcome any new internal Family Members that revealed themselves. Notice if your awareness of your body is different after this experience.

Drop into a relaxed state in which all of your body is relaxed, and your breath is easy. Read the following slowly, staying in connection with your system.

IMAGINE

Imagine you awaken one day, after a deep and restful night's sleep, to find you are not in your bed, but in a comfortable nest made of large, soft leaves with a soft, puffy, oversized flower blossom for a pillow. As you open your eyes to a translucent morning light peering through the leaves, you notice that the light is coming from not one, but five different suns, all slightly different pastel colors, beaming gently onto the landscape. The air smells sweet and fresh.

Just as you think of rising, your nest is suddenly floating on a peaceful lake reflecting an iridescent purple color. The water is clear, and you jump in for a dip. All over your body, champagne bubbles form, making it a lively swim. As you draw closer to shore, you see a golden, pink and azure fire, with people dancing, cooking, and singing. The texture under your feet is like a cloud as you walk out of the water. The bright sound of unfamiliar birds fills the air, and the colors in the sky change with each call.

Let yourself rest in this place, and allow all of your senses to fill with a world beyond your imagination.

ACKNOWLDGEMENTS

The creation of this book was a long process. To the many who offered words of encouragement and support along the way, I am deeply grateful. Specifically, I would like to thank Jeff Carreira for providing the initial invitation for this adventure, Suzanne Potts for her pivotal work with me in the early stages of creation, Winna Hostetler for her relentless encouragement and valuable feedback, Yvonne Philpott for her honesty and clarity in proof reading, and John Elder for his incisive critique in the final stages.

Mahalo Nui Loa to Ho'okahi (Tamara Stephens) for her support and guidance over the years, Auntie Pi'ilani Rupert for her loving encouragement, and scholar Pono Fried for advising me around use of Hawaiian language and cultural practices. You are all beacons to me in wonderfully diverse ways. Thank you for your Presence in helping me allow this dream to come true.

I also wish to acknowledge all the participants who have attended Retreats with Lineage of Light throughout the years. Mahalo for your willingness to step with me into the magical world of this Pathway. The container, holding each person and each unique Retreat experience springing from the 'call' you each sent out, has been my teacher.

To all my Assistants, Organizers and hosts, including, Santhe Tanner, Grace O'Riordan, Eva Lennox, Caragh Munn, Kekoa Powers, Cher Vrieling, Kara Jo French, Sarabeth Rings, Susan Hoffmann, Yvonne Philpott, Andre Levine & The Lotus Heart Centre, Carine van den Berg, Thomas Primas & Mario Benetti of the Kientalerhof 'Ohana, Sonja and Carie of the Boghill 'Ohana, Fred and Yanni Weiler, Elvira & Heinz of Artistirma, Angel Costa, and Mackensie Grant. You have been the ground on which this work could be shared in the world. Myself, and all who have benefitted, have you to thank.

I leave you with an excerpt of a poem, by Rabindranath Tagore from 'A Flight of Swans', which has reverberated through me since the beginning of this profound journey:

I hear the countless voices of the human heart
Flying unseen,
From the dim past to the dim unblossomed future.
Hear, within my own breast,
The fluttering of the homeless bird, which,
In company with countless others,
Flies day and night,
Through light and darkness,
From shore to shore unknown.
The void of the universe is resounding with the music of wings:
"Not here, not here, somewhere far beyond."

GLOSSARY

Simple translations of Hawaiian words
For deeper study, consult the Hawaiian Dictionary
by Mary Kawaena Pukui & Samuel H. Elbert

Aliʻi ʻAimoku Title of a Ruling Chief in ancient Hawaiʻi

Auaʼia, Makaʼiʼole, Titles of accomplishment similar to Masters Degree &
ʻuliamaʼ Doctorate

Heiau Ancient temple structure of Hawaiʼi

Hoʼoponopono A healing practice of ancient Hawaiʼi designed to bring relationships with ourselves and others into balance, harmony and forgiveness.

Kahuna Master / Expert in a field or fields of study

Kāhuna Plural of Kahuna

Kalo Taro plant. First born relative of the Hawaiian people in the Hawaiian Creation Story

Kaona Hidden meaning originally applied to oral and then written language such as chant, poetry, story or sacred teachings. Similar to allegory or symbolic representation found in modern literature.

Kauaʻi Northernmost inhabited island of the Hawaiian archipelago

Ke Ahi Pū Female version of awakening Life Force energy (Kundalini)

Ke Ala Hōkū ʻThe Pathway to The Starsʼ

Ke Nu'u Ma Mao Male version of awakening Life Force energy (Kundalini)

Kukui A native tree most widely known throughout Polynesia as a source of light using the oily nut of the tree.

Lua Hawaiian martial art

Mana Life Force Energy

Moloka'i Island in the Hawaiian archipelago

'Ohana Family

'Ohana Nui The Great Family of all living beings

Papa Earth Mother of the Hawaiian Creation Story

Romi Kaparere 'To dance around the table' Kahu's form of bodywork which he previously called 'Kahuna Bodywork'

Wākea Sky Father of the Hawaiian Creation Story

www.ingramcontent.com/pod-product-compliance
Lightning Source LLC
Chambersburg PA
CBHW062115080426

42734CB00012B/2872